MAGICAL KNOWLEDGE

BOOK THREE

CONTACTS OF THE ADEPTS

BY JOSEPHINE MCCARTHY

SECOND EDITION

TaDehent Books
Exeter
2020

Copyright 2020 © Josephine McCarthy

All rights reserved

Without limiting the rights under copyright reserved above, no part of this publication may be reproduced, stored in, or introduced into a retrieval system, or transmitted, in any form or by any means (electronic, mechanical, photocopying, recording or otherwise) without prior permission of the copyright owner and the publisher of this book.

First edition published by Mandrake of Oxford, 2012

Second edition published by TaDehent Books 2020
Exeter UK

ISBN 978-1-911134-52-7

Cover image by Stuart Littlejohn
Typeset by Michael Sheppard

Dedicated to
RA (Bob) Gilbert
and
Stuart Littlejohn

with special thanks to Jon and Andrea

Contents

Introduction   1

1 Methods of working with temples and deities   5
    1.1 Deities: working practice and power dynamics   6
    1.2 Working with Deities in the Temple Environment   8
    1.3 Finding the Doorway   9
    1.4 Creating a window for the deity 10
    1.5 Work on site or move the site? How to move a Temple . . 14
    1.6 The difference between a deity and Divinity in a magical temple space 19
    1.7 Visionary ritual action 20
    1.8 Visionary movement 23
    1.9 Summary 25

2 The magic of the fire/volcanic temple   27
    2.1 The use of volcanic magic 28
    2.2 The path to working with volcanic/fire power 29
    2.3 Visions of the volcanic temples 30
    2.4 Going into the city beneath the waves 31
    2.5 The cave in the centre of the world that links all volcanoes 36
    2.6 The vision of the cave 40
    2.7 The contact of the sword maker 43
    2.8 The work with swords 44
    2.9 The vision of the sword maker 45

3 The power and magic of utterance, sound and sigil   51
    3.1 Vision: the mediation of sound at the edge of the Abyss . 55
    3.2 Utterance in the temple 58
    3.3 The vision of utterance in the temple 60
    3.4 The vision for the creation of magical sigils 63
    3.5 Working with the sacred sigils and alphabet 67
    3.6 Sacred alphabet 68

4 The magical dynamics of fate — 71
- 4.1 Vision of the conception of a soul out in the stars 74
- 4.2 Chess and the Inner Temple 76
- 4.3 The board game 77
- 4.4 Summary 87

5 How to work with angels: bound, religious, part human and natural — 89
- 5.1 Bound angels 90
- 5.2 Religious angels 93
- 5.3 The consecration of the cathedral 95
- 5.4 Religious angels of recitation 97
- 5.5 The vision of recitation 97
- 5.6 Human angels 100
- 5.7 Sandalphon/Synadalphos ("colleague") 101
- 5.8 Vision of the Companion 101
- 5.9 Metatron 103
- 5.10 The vision of Metatron and the Abyss 104
- 5.11 Natural angels 106
- 5.12 The vision of the Metatron Cube 107
- 5.13 The Archon and the Aeon 113
- 5.14 Working advice 114
- 5.15 Vision of the pattern of death 114

6 Practical methods for creating ritual tools — 117
- 6.1 Consecration of tools in the deepest part of the temple .. 117
- 6.2 Consecration ritual/vision for a consecrated Sword of Justice 118
- 6.3 Ritually enlivening the scabbard 123
- 6.4 Placing a being within the sword 127
- 6.5 Bridging a being into a tool 128
- 6.6 Awakening Divinity in substance 129
- 6.7 Summary 132

7 The magic of the Underworld — 133
- 7.1 Vision of the Goddess in the Cave and her presence in the Abyss 136
- 7.2 The Sisters at the back of the North Wind 141
- 7.3 Vision of the Sisters at the back of the North Wind 142
- 7.4 Origins of humanity in the Abyss 148
- 7.5 Methods of descent 152

8 Functioning as an adept — 155
- 8.1 Service 156

	8.2	Practicalities of living as an adept 160
	8.3	Working within a tradition 162
	8.4	The future: passing on the teaching 163

A Advanced Decoys   167
     A.1   Personal decoys 168
     A.2   False doors 170
     A.3   Time decoys 172
     A.4   Oppositions 175
     A.5   Copper as deflection 177

B The prehistory of magical development: a series of unfortunate events   179
     B.1   Magic and its forms 181
     B.2   The series of unfortunate events 183
     B.3   People and responses 187
     B.4   Early ritual solar circles 193
     B.5   Chambered tombs in Northern Europe 199

Introduction

The Contacts of the Adepts is a book that will hopefully act as a springboard for those who have spent a great deal of time learning, doing and exploring the inner realms and ritual magical patterns. This book holds more visions that the other two books, because this phase of a magical life is more about doing inner work in vision and visionary ritual/magical actions, than learning or practising. It was very difficult to decide what should actually go into this book, not because of censorship, but because there is just so much material, so many directions and so many contacts out there: the book would be too large and would be like working with a feral teenager. I have chosen areas of work that need the most attention and focused upon the most active contacts within those subject areas. You will notice, once you get to the end of the book, that the different areas of magic and the various contacts within the visions interconnect and interweave: in truth, they are all of one another.

I have approached certain key elements of the inner realms from various different angles within the book, giving you a chance to have a much more in-depth understanding of important patterns and contacts within the inner realms. For example, in the book there are various different visions and contacts that bring the practitioner into contact with the Metatron Cube, a key pattern of consciousness within the inner realms, and something that truly needs to be understood if you really want to work magically at any depth. By approaching it this way, you begin to see how different roads often lead to the same place, and that which road you approach it from dictates how it will present and interact with you.

Working at an adept level means working in depth in the Inner Worlds and bringing that work out into the physical world through ritual, utterance and focused thought. The rituals become less and less elaborate and more powerful in their action, with a simple ritual bringing deep and lasting change into the world. Because the power levels become so intense, the adept has to be a clear and focused window, through which ancient consciousness can flow without the interference of agenda, dogma and limited emotive intelligence.

To achieve this level of mediation, the adept needs to have worked in all the worlds, learned about the beings and about themselves. The learning about yourself is key to success in magical work: the ancient saying of "man, know thyself" never ages and fits a great deal of wisdom into three words. To truly know your weaknesses and be willing to confront them, to challenge yourself and be able to make yourself do the right thing, and be as unselfish as possible, is the real key to magical success. The reason for this is not psychological, it is plain common sense: if you know what your weaknesses are and address them, then powerful destructive beings cannot get a true hold on you and destroy you.

The other major step that brings a magician to adeptship is truly absorbing the Mysteries of death-in-life. To work in death, to walk through death and be totally at home in that realm with no fear, brings a human into direct contact with the deeper eternal side of themselves. The fear of death falls away and the true understanding of how the cycles work emerge into the daily consciousness of the person. The knowledge of who you really are, and what you bring into the manifest world filters through into your everyday consciousness, enabling you to mature beyond being a student into being a worker.

Similarly the work in the Inner Desert brings us to the foot of Divine Consciousness without all the religious dressing. We experience Divinity as a power, and the structure of life for what it is. That enables us to work with those powers as coworkers and not as religious devotees who are dependant upon the whims of deities and the traps of religious dogmas. Divinity is constantly renewing itself and we are a part of that process. Whether we are an active participant in that process or a passive pawn depends upon whether we are willing to pick up the spade and start shovelling rather than standing before the pile of shit and praying for someone else to do it for us. All of these things turn a neophyte into an adept, not exams, studying texts and wearing fancy robes. Magic is real life, not dressing up and playing fantasy games, and when we finally realize that, we step forward into a world that is beyond anything we could have dreamed of. That is the step of the Adept.

With the net, the gift of Anu, held close to his side, he himself raised up IMHULLU the atrocious wind, the tempest, the whirlwind, the hurricane, the wind of four and the wind of seven, the tumid wind worst of all.

— The magical battle between Marduk and Tiamat.

Chapter One

Methods of working with temples and deities

The work of the outer temple for an adept is a complex and yet clear mix of communing, moving power, creating and destroying. By the time a magician gets to an advanced level of work, the two roads of ritual and visionary magic come together to create a mega highway of power: neither of the two methods can work in an advanced form without the other: one fuels the action, the other gives it form. And yet one can separate them out as an individual action, but in truth, once the work gets to this level each form has fragments of the other within it. So for example, it becomes very hard to work a ritual where you are not also drawing the Inner Worlds into the ritual, hence melding the two together. Similarly in vision, what becomes apparent is that the deeper in vision you go at this level, the more ritualized your outer motions become before, during and after the vision. So for example where a visionary magician may think he or she is only doing a vision, they will find themselves ritualizing the visionary space, working with their hands while in vision (sigil forming and power weaving) and ritualizing the close-down afterwards.

What becomes apparent from this is that the closer to power you get, the less formalized the *dressing* of the action becomes: a ritual becomes less about outfits, wand waving and long speeches, and more about focused movement/action, true utterance and enlivening. Visionary structures become less about the description and detail, and more about sensation and focused image. The further from the surface and the deeper into the inner realms you go, the less identifiable the form becomes so that you end up working with a power source instead of a deity or magical structure. For example, where a magician may be used to 'seeing' certain 'places' and beings

1. Methods of working with temples and deities

while working in vision, as they move deeper into the inner realms, the forms all fall away and the magician instead sees nothing, but feels the presence and the power. Sometimes the magician may lose all senses altogether and go into a sleep-like state. But they are not sleeping: they have gone beyond what the conscious mind can cope with so the subconscious kicks in, which in turn cuts out the conscious use of the imagination: they go into the deepest form of consciousness. They will awaken on cue and often not remember anything that happened. However when the need for specific skills or information arises, anything that was 'downloaded' into the magician during that sleep state will reemerge ready to for use. Such a state can often also bring about profound changes within the magician which will manifest in their everyday lives.

The very interesting dynamic is that when you move deeper and work with the more formless magic, you are more able to work in the complexity of the surface manifestation/ritual while retaining the power levels of the deeper contact: you bring the two together. Always, magic is about opposites, tension and polarities, and that works through every single layer, angle, presentation and being.

1.1 Deities: working practice and power dynamics

A word of caution before we go any further: working with deities demands a very open mind in many ways. You are potentially stretching back to a completely different culture and a totally different way of thinking. One of the problems with the magical lines today is the subtle sexist attitudes in certain lines of magic. The Golden Dawn, for all the good it did in giving magic a wider audience, also perpetuated an odd attitude towards women. Even though they were revolutionary in their time in their attitude towards women, the way that the system was built and operates subtly encourages an imbalance in the polarities which is evident to this day in many Golden Dawn magicians. They also created limitations upon the magic i.e. the lack of trained visionary work and overdramatized ritual are problems that are still embedded within the mindset to this day. Crowley then picked up on this and ran with it, creating

1.1. Deities: working practice and power dynamics

even more of an imbalance while further dismissing the concept of controlled vision in magic.

People who have come up through these magical lines are going to have inherited some pretty limited and unbalanced ways of thinking. If you approach some of these ancient priests and priestesses with such a mindset, they will destroy you. Trust me, the priestesses of some of these ancient temples (and I mean ancient, not 100 B.C., more like 4000 B.C.) are powerful, bloodthirsty and are built, power-wise, like brick shithouse walls. If you carry mental attitudes about women being inferior and weak, they will tear you to pieces. That limited, arrogant mindset traces all the way back to ancient Greece and even a bit earlier than that. It was a propaganda campaign that was perpetuated to muzzle the destroying warrior goddesses who had gotten out of balance: times were changing, cultures where changing and solar male kingship was ascendant.

But the same could also be said regarding women going into the inner world temples: if you go in with a hostile attitude towards men, or a derogatory attitude, the male priesthood will tear you apart: it's all about respect and balance. Both sexes have power, they are different in their magical expressions, but bring the two together in a working environment and you have a potentially massive expanse of magic. In the ancient temples, discussion and patience are not qualities that most of the inner contacts have: you have to be neutral and be able to chameleon to the mindset of the powers you are working with. That way you do not clash head-on. Before we get back to the magic, I want to tell you a little story that perfectly highlights what can go wrong, then I promise I will end my lecture on sexism. This is a true and very sad story about how magical work can go wrong if you have the wrong attitude.

Many years ago, I was working alongside a group of experienced magicians in Bath, England. The house where we were working was directly over part of the ancient temple to the goddess Sul, a dark Underworld goddess (not a goddess of the sun, as some moron has put up on the web). We had opened the gates to the Inner Worlds and we were taking turns talking to this powerful Goddess and preparing to do deeper service work with her.

1. Methods of Working with Temples and Deities

One of the magicians, when it came to his turn to communicate with her, stood arrogantly in vision before her. She took out a blade and put it to his throat. This is a common challenge that a Dark Goddess does to men—besides ripping off their testicles, which is one of her favourites: this is not about neutering, but about changing and deepening power.

Instead of standing still, submitting to her challenge and trusting her, he knocked the blade to one side and challenged her to a fight. (Ouch!) When he came out of the vision, he was very full of himself and would not be told that such action was indeed very stupid, and that he would suffer consequences: she is a destroying goddess, her job is to destroy you. If you trust her, she will do it in a way that clears all of your crap away ready for regeneration. If you do not trust her, she will just destroy you. And that is exactly what she did.

On his way home, he had an epileptic seizure. He was not epileptic and had never had problems before: he was in the peak of heath. He was taken to hospital. He had another, and another. It ended up with him losing his job, his home, his driver's license, and he suffered frequent fits and minor brain damage. She destroyed him for his lack of respect. If he had let her challenge him and do whatever she needed to do, she would have sent things into his life that would have changed how he thought, how he did things: she would have put life experience in his way that would have been hard, but she would also have destroyed the parts of him that were holding him back.

These powers are real. It is not a game, and if you break into contact with them, they will mediate power to you that does a job. That is what they are there for. And that is why people built temples to them and worked with them, not because of fear and superstition, but because these beings could influence their daily lives and help with natural disasters.

1.2 Working with Deities in the Temple Environment

This is a very delicate line of magical work that has to be trodden very carefully and thoughtfully. As a magician, it is very important right at the outset of work with a deity that you establish a working relationship and not a worship relationship. If you are working in a temple environment as opposed to a magical space, which is different, then it is even more important to tread carefully, as the line between religion and practical magic comes very close. But the difference is still there and must be adhered to, unless you want to spend the rest of your life chained to one line of work without the possibility of parole.

The reason it is so much more dangerous in a temple is that a temple structure has deeper power foundations than a magical space and often many beings within its inner structure. So the power levels, contacts and doorways are at a much more aggressive power level, and there is usually a doorway through which the deity can cross over the threshold into the outer space.

Keeping all that in mind, work in a temple with a deity usually takes the form of visionary ritual, and visionary ritual movement. Remember at all times that the deity is a powerful working companion, teacher and sometimes parent, but they are not to be treated as all-powerful gods and goddesses to whom you swear allegiance, agree with totally, or give anything that is asked of you. Keep this line very clear in your own head and in your work.

1.3 Finding the Doorway

The best way to learn about working with a deity in a temple environment is to first work with them in an ancient temple if you have access to one. This would include stone circles, ancient ruins and power spots that are known to have been worked with. Some will have been shut down ritually, and if that is the case then I would suggest that you let sleeping dogs lie. If they are not shut down then the first step is to find out where the 'access' gate is. That will be an area in the structure that acted as a gateway for the deity in the absence of a statue. Every temple has one: it is just a matter of finding it. Do not trust ancient scripts or maps of the temple when it was still active: often the true gateway was hidden from the public eye and was heavily guarded.

The best way to find the doorway is to sit as close to the centre of the temple as you can get and light a candle flame. Fire was used

1. Methods of working with temples and deities

in about ninety percent of ancient temples, so it is the easiest way to switch the lights on. (Unless you are very unlucky and happen to have chosen one of the rare temples that did not use fire.) If the candle flame is lit using inner technique, i.e. also seeing the inner flame, then there is a major possibility it will switch on all the lights, which will make your attempt a whole lot easier. With the flame before you, sit with your eyes closed and using your inner vision and imagination, look to each direction around the site. Then see yourself getting up and walking around the site, looking in all the corners and directions. Be patient: this is a skill that needs time to develop, and the echo of the doorway may be very faint. But you will, if it is still there, pick up on it. There will be an area that feels or looks 'different', welcoming or energetic. That will be the area that housed the doorway.

Once that is established, put out the candle and go have a look around that area. If it is a temple complex you may find fragments of the old altar or the actual point where the focus was for the deity. If it is a stone circle or complex, there will just be an area that was a doorway and getting as close as possible to that will be sufficient.

If you live close to the site, go regularly and build up the power of the doorway before moving onto doing actual 'work': the more solid the door, the easier the rest of the work will be. If you do not live close and have only a limited timeframe to work in, then it would be an idea to build a 'window' for the deity, which means having a vessel and connecting that vessel to the deity. The doorway is used as a threshold for the deity to bring them through, and then the deity is connected into a vessel that can be taken away. This vessel will act as a 'window' for the deity so that they can interact with you wherever your ritual space is. It is a weaker alternative to actually moving the whole temple pattern, which is discussed later in this chapter.

1.4 Creating a window for the deity

Whatever site you are working with, you will need to have something that can be used as a focal substance for the deity so that you can take it away with you if you want to carry on working with the deity away from the temple site. This can be anything from a statue or image of the deity, to a stone that is used as either the doorway or as

1.4. Creating a window for the deity

an altar. If you are trying to contact one of the deities at the stone circles I would suggest that you do not use an image or statue, even if it is homemade: those powers had no images that we know of and certainly none exist to this day, so to give that deity a pair of eyes and a mouth may be a very big mistake. We have no clear knowledge of what they were and what they did, so working with a stone will be a safer filter until you really get to know what the deity's agenda is. For example, they may be a power form that demands a human life in return for working with you. If you refuse, they may take one anyhow, and they will only be able to see the lives that are attached to you (lovers, children etc). Those ancient deities can be very dangerous, so really, tread carefully.

If you are working in an ancient temple site, then chances are you already know background information of the deity there. There may be a possibility, depending on what temple you are in, that the deity has been bound there, or has had limits placed upon them. If the temple is after 1500 B.C. then there is a good chance that there is no binding or inner interference. Either those abilities were slowly lost over time or that action was just stopped, as such bindings seem to fade around 1500 B.C..

You have identified the area of the temple where the doorway is. The next step is to open it. Some temples can be still 'up and running' from an inner point of view, and the minute you take an inner step towards the doorway, all the lights will go on and all the people will stream out, which can be a little bit disconcerting. Others have been shut or have gradually closed down over the millennia, and there is no easy way to differentiate, so tread carefully.

The first attempt should be purely using inner imaginary techniques. Imagine two pillars creating a gateway with two flames before them. See beyond the pillars a deep mist. Using your inner voice, call upon the deity and ask them to grace the temple once more. If everything in the temple is still active, then this simple imaginary action will be enough to trigger a contact. It might take a few minutes and you may have to also use your breath, i.e. speak the summons out loud (the power of utterance). The way to know that you have a real contact is your body will react with being so close to a deity. If that works, then talk to the deity and tell them your intentions, of your wish to work with them. If the temple is not close to where

1. METHODS OF WORKING WITH TEMPLES AND DEITIES

you live, explain this and ask if they are willing to work with an image/statue/object as an interface that you can take home with you.

If that simple inner exchange does not work, then you will need to exteriorize some of it. Find two reasonably large stones and create a doorway with them. Light two candles (tea lights in jam jars are good to work with) and again create a doorway, or one light in the centre. Repeat the inner exercise, whilst also calling upon the gate keepers to open the gates, and ask the deity to come back into our world. The two together makes for a much stronger action: just remember that verbal and ritual action alone without inner action will not work at all unless it is an exact replica of what was used in the temple (which will trigger the inner pattern). As the deity appears in inner vision, prick your finger and place a drop of blood upon the statue, image or stone that will be the focus for the deity. That will provide the deity with a connection to you and will also provide fuel.

The next step, after introducing yourself and explaining your intentions, will be to bridge the deity into the object, if they agree to the action. Because you are in the temple where they were housed and at the threshold of the doorway, a whole load of work that would usually have to be done to open a window to a deity into an object is unnecessary. You simply have to provide the bridge for the deity, which you do using your own body. Once you are ready, turn your back to the deity and place your hands upon the receiving object, and using your inner vision, 'see' the deity behind you and feel their power building up. The deity will step into you and then through you, passing through your body and into the object. They will then pass through the object, leaving a trail that looks a bit like a tunnel through you and the object.

What has been done is that by passing through you and the object, the deity has created a change within both you and the object that will make it much easier for the deity to use both you and the object as a window. It's like placing a mark upon you, and a window inside you and the object, so that they can commune and see through you/the object into the outside world. Once it is finished, then you can put the lights out and leave. If the deity has bindings upon them, or if there are still guarded boundaries around the temple, you may find it very hard to get the object out of the temple. A whole variety of things can happen from the power suddenly vanishing out of the object,

1.4. Creating a window for the deity

from you dropping and breaking the image, to someone arriving and stopping you, to feeling sick or suddenly drained.

If there are just guardians, you may make it home but after a couple of nights of bad nightmares and sudden illness, you may be forced to take the object back or destroy it. If these restrictions do appear, heed their warnings and do not, under any circumstances ignore what is happening. They are usually there for a good reason, usually because the deity is/was far too dangerous to be out in the world at large. If this happens, take the object back and bury it somewhere within the temple. You will only be able to work face-to-face with the deity while you are in the actual temple. If they are a deity that has a much larger field than the local area, i.e. they are a god/ess of the Sun etc., then this will probably not happen and you should be able to work and bring them through anywhere.

If they are specific to an area, hill, spring etc., then they may well be bound to that area either naturally or by magic. Don't try to take that on and 'free' them: you could be responsible for committing mass murder or chaos if you do, or the other outcome may be that you kill yourself or are sent mad (the two usual outcomes of clashing with inner power).

The basic rule of thumb is know your deity and if they are very localized, then you have to understand, before you start to try and commune with them, that you may not be able to work with them at home: you will have to travel to the temple to work with them. (Although some localized deities do seem to travel well, so it is not a hard and fast rule: much of this work is about experimenting.) Also, if at all possible, look as far back in records as you can to find out about them. Do not take the more recent myths about them at face value, as they are usually manipulated: go back to the very early stories where you are most likely to get a truer picture. And keep that picture in mind when you start to work with them. And don't forget: if they were magically shut down, it may have been for a very good reason.

1. METHODS OF WORKING WITH TEMPLES AND DEITIES

1.5 Work on site or move the site? How to move a Temple

Once you have established a contact on site at the temple, the next decision has to be whether to build up the work onsite or 'move' the site. What makes a temple powerful is its inner structure, which can be moved (by a strong group of people) if necessary. This is something that needs a group of able magicians, all of whom need to have varying degrees of inner 'sight.' You will also need four ballast workers who will guard the perimeter while you work. The other thing that you will need is a 'temple' to house the inner structure once you move it. You can use an already standing building, but then you run many risks of contamination of the site by its other users, and also losing control over the building itself. (Plus you really do not want to have the Temple of Set in your living room.) It is best to choose a spot of land or a field that is never used, or that you own, and mark out boundaries with stones. The temple will nestle its boundary pattern into the stones. If you own a building that you can limit access to, then it could be a suitable vessel.

You do not need to be at the site to do this work, but you do need something, just a stone, from the site to act as a resonant focus. I have moved a small site, and we as a group were not physically onsite, but we had all visited. It was extremely hard physical work and we all had extreme strain afterwards, but we did it and it worked well.

You need to have visited the site physically so that your body remembers the frequency of the place. If you can be all physically in the temple space, then the physical strain is kept to a minimum and the work will be far more successful. This technique is basically an extension of the technique used for taking the consecrated implement out of the physical implement and putting it into something else.

The room or space which will be the receiving vessel should be prepared, with an altar space that will mark the doorway for the deity, a defined entrance for the workers, and a central working position for whoever is leading the work. For this working, the altar should have two candles that will mark the doorway, and also two candles for the person leading: one on either side of them. The use of fire in creating doorways is ancient and powerful, hence its removal by the

1.5. Work on site or move the site? How to move a Temple

Protestant church. (It is interesting to note that the magical patterns that have been born out of Freemasonry, which in turn was affected by the Protestant leanings of its members, also did not use flames in a magical way, making life far more difficult for them.)

The number of workers you will need is twelve for the perimeter and one for the centre, along with the four guardians who will provide ballast. The perimeter workers need to be equally distributed around the working space and beyond them, four ballast workers who will sit one in each direction outside of the working pattern. Their job is simply to guard the space from any interference. This will mean they need to be in vision in the room, just watching. Sometimes, the power of this work will attract people to the space and they will try to enter. Again, the job of the guardians is to intercept such intrusions.

The person who sits in the centre, who is the fulcrum, leads the work. Either side of her is a candle that is tuned to be access gates for inner workers. The fulcrum leads a vision that takes the workers down into the Underworld and emerges back up to the surface in the temple site back in time when it was recently built. The workers are able to observe the inner patterns of the temple construct and watch as its power flows around the space. The fulcrum then leads the workers to the inner sanctum of the temple, where the power source and doorway of the deity is. The fulcrum calls upon the deity and as the deity appears (sometimes they are there waiting) the fulcrum explains to the deity what the group is trying to achieve and why. They then ask the deity if they are willing to assist and to allow their temple to be moved. If the deity agrees, then first each worker must introduce themselves to the deity and be 'touched' by the deity. This is a subtle form of tying in energetically with the deity so that the body of the worker can be upheld and supported by the deity during the work.

Once everyone has had their turn in communion with the deity, then it is time to begin the process of removal. The deity will turn and lead the fulcrum, and the workers will follow as the deity steps back through the doorway. The deity leads the group out onto the plains of the Inner Desert, with the Abyss in one direction and the River of Death in the other. The group is led to the edge of the Abyss, then prompted to turn and look back over the Inner Desert. The pattern of the temple appears before them in the Inner Desert with the deity

1. Methods of Working with Temples and Deities

standing the middle. The pattern is the lines of angelic consciousness that make up the inner power structure that the temple was then built around. It appears as a series of interlocking patterns and Platonic solids that give off a barely detectable sound. The deity stands in the middle and acts as a central point of balance to the whole structure. The fulcrum is then summoned to the deity and told to walk 'into' the deity, assuming the central role of balance.

The workers take up positions around the pattern and upon prompt from the fulcrum, take a thread of the pattern that anchors it into the ground of the Inner Desert. When everyone is ready, the workers begin to wind in the pattern, like gathering up threads of wool. It is important that the workers all work at the same speed, and it is up to the fulcrum, who is leading the vision, to ensure that everyone works at the same pace. One way to do this is to time each roll of thread verbally while still in vision (i.e. and now roll to a count of three then wait, and repeat). In visions, the threads are rolled and placed in the arms of the fulcrum who is then immediately upheld by the group. To uphold the fulcrum, the moment the worker hands the roll of thread to the fulcrum, the worker then places (in vision) a hand upon the fulcrum and leaves it there. This ensures that the burden, which is heavy indeed (being the weight of angelic consciousness), is upheld by the whole group. As each person touches the fulcrum, they must state out loud that they are finished. This is for the benefit of the guardians.

The moment that the pattern is bound up, any demonic guardians that were employed to guard the temple will appear. The fact that the group is working with the deity ensures that the group will be safe from attack, but the demonic beings will need to be redeployed in the temple once it is unfurled. When the guardians hear the last call from the workers, they must then be ready to 'buddy up' with the demonic guardians while the temple is being re-sited. For the guardians, they will experience a sudden heaviness or strain as they uphold the demonic guardians. The fulcrum, speaking from within the deity, will tell the demonic beings to go and sit with the guardians while the temple structure is being re-sited.

The fulcrum, still within the deity and holding the burden of the pattern, leads the group down the path of the Inner Desert, over the threshold of Malkuth (manifestation) and into the life pattern of the

1.5. Work on site or move the site? How to move a Temple

fulcrum. The fulcrum walks through their life pattern (like taking a walk down a path of your life as an observer, a very weird experience indeed) until they get to the point of the working in the room. Once back in the room where they first started, the fulcrum holds her arms out and calls to the workers to take and unfold the pattern that they were working with, and to anchor it in the land. The workers each call out when they are finished. When the last worker has called out, then the demonic guardians are asked to take up position once more in the pattern, guarding the directions and the doorway.

The fulcrum will stand and walk towards the area of the new housing that will accommodate the doorway for the deity, and if there is an altar, they will place their hands up on it. The deity will then pull away from the fulcrum and take up residence in the doorway. The fulcrum then describes the inner pattern and the outer temple in the vision, so that the whole group has the same imagery, which is imprinted upon the room, and the deity is thanked and welcomed.

The group comes out of vision and the two candles of the doorway are lit. The guardians wait as the workers and the fulcrum leave the room, and then the guardians are the last to leave. The candles are left burning and the room is left empty so that the inner structure can embed itself in the space. From now on, that space is used as the original temple and it must be worked with daily for the pattern to strengthen and settle. Eventually—and there is no telling how long the embedding phase will take, it can be anything from a few days to a few weeks or even months sometimes—it will have settled, and then it can be worked with less frequently, so long as it is regular.

★ ★ ★

As you can see, this working method utilizes the method of working both in vision and ritually at the same time. The workers, while in vision, also have to be able to call out with their voices at certain junctions in the work, so that timings can be communicated. This means that each worker must be able to work in vision without drifting or falling asleep: they have to be fully conscious all the way through the working. This can be achieved by having the workers stand through the vision. An extension of this could be to have the workers ritually moving through the vision i.e. during the rolling of

1. Methods of working with temples and deities

the threads, etc. Either way, this technique demands a high level of concentration and discipline in the participating magicians.

One of the things that will become very apparent from very early on from working in this transferred temple is the reality of what the temple's original magical pattern was, and what was overlaid dogma or interference at the original site. When you move a temple structure using the above method, you are moving the bare skeletal energetic structure that the temple hung upon, not all the layers of human interference, agenda and magical manipulations. You are down to the very basic foundation that allows the deity to flow through and work with humanity unhindered. Most ancient temples will have many layers to them, and many of those layers will be magically bound, triggered, and manipulated.

By working with the sheer skeletal structure, you create the doorway for the deity while bypassing all the following generations of priestly interference, binding and pinning that became so common in powerful temples by around 1500 B.C.. What will be left at the original site will simply be the patterns of consciousness that grew over the years of work that happened on that site, but the original inner infrastructure of the temple, the 'inner template of the temple' will no longer be there: that is what you move, and this is what you rebuild and work with. Without that inner structure, the original site of the temple simply becomes an outer shell, and the consciousness patterns will naturally degrade and slowly vanish.

When you begin to work with the deity in this reformed temple, keep very tight records of every interaction, every working and every communication with the deity so that a complete picture of that deity can be built up. Most of what we read from later wall paintings and historical texts is often misleading. You will often find that when you work this way, you will experience the deity in a form that is similar to the very early descriptions by ancient priests. The longer the temple is around, the more manipulated and changed the story becomes.

If for any reason your site has to be abandoned, then you must rewind the temple structure back up and take it out into the Inner Desert and let it unfurl there (and don't forget the demonic beings). If you leave the structure unguarded and unworked with, it can become 'feral' as it will have not had decades of work to stabilize it. This can become dangerous and all sorts of things can go wrong—and the fulcrum will bear the energetic brunt of what goes wrong. So if the temple is to be abandoned for any reason, take it into the Inner Desert and preferably wind it into the deity so that they absorb the structure.

Such work carries a great deal of responsibility, as so many things can go wrong (or right). If you plan to do this work, ensure that you are planning to work with and evolve the structure over decades, and be willing to carry the burden of work should the temple need to be dismantled.

However, if it is worked with and cared for by successive generations, then you will find that the temple will slowly build, particularly if you connect it up to the Inner Library, and it will become a place where adepts will come to work after death. With such care, these temples often take on a life of their own and grow to become vast areas of learning, work and magic, which can serve generations to come.

If there should be a need to build an inner and outer temple from scratch, then the techniques to such work can be found in my book *The Work of the Hierophant* (Golem Media).

1.6 The difference between a deity and Divinity in a magical temple space

One very important difference that is often overlooked in the magical space of a temple is the very big difference between a deity and Divinity in working practice. I have harped on about this difference *ad nauseam* in my writings, simply because so few magicians stop to think about the distinctions and how that difference affects their work.

When you are working in a temple space with a deity, the deity is going to dictate, to an extent (even if they are not 'worshipped') how the temple operates, what line of magic is undertaken and how that magic is ritually approached. So if you bring a deity to work with you into a magical temple, be aware that even if the deity is working with you as a coworker, it will limit certain aspects of your magical freedom. This is partly to do with the characteristics of the deity, their defined area of interest and the areas of their expertise. A deity is not an all-powerful, all-knowing being: they have limitations like the rest of us, and they also have very distinct agendas. They will steer the work of the temple to fit their agenda if they are allowed to.

If you bring a deity into the temple to work, or you create a doorway within the temple for that consciousness, then you will only be able to work magic in areas that are conducive to that deity. If you are wishing to work in many different areas of magic over time, then bringing a specific deity into the temple space in such a way is not a very bright idea. If however you are wishing to develop long-term work in a very defined area of magic, then having a deity along for the ride that is very involved in that area of work will truly enhance any long-term projects and make the job a whole lot easier.

For complex and contrasting magical work over a protracted length of time, it is more advisable to work directly with Divinity, which takes on a more formless, but infinitely more powerful pattern, and is simply mediated into the space from the central flame. The downside (if it *is* a downside of working this way) is that you have far less control over the magic that you work with, and you become somewhat of an active observer to the magic as opposed to its instigator and controller. This method of working in the magical temple is best for long-term service work or very large projects that affect a great many people or the land. But if your work is more about a localized area, fertility, small projects, or individuals, then it is far better and a lot easier to work with deities or with neither.

1.7 Visionary ritual action

What follows sort of sounds like fancy New Age self-healing therapy. Thankfully, it is not. It is a working method for moving power around and for effecting change. The basic, stripped-down working method is to open the gateway and call the deity into the temple space. Once the deity is on the threshold of the temple space, turn with your back to the deity and using vision and utterance, call the deity into yourself or to join you in action. They will put their arms through your arms so that you work together. Usually, for this type of technique, you would have before you a miniature model or drawing of what you

1.7. Visionary ritual action

want to work on. You use your mind, breath and arm actions, with the deity working through you as a power source, to effect change over the model, which is magically linked to the real place/person.

For example, let's take a situation that is happening as I write this chapter. A large earthquake and subsequent tsunami has just hit Japan (today is the thirteenth of March) and one of the reactors has just exploded. If this was to be worked with in the temple setting, it would go something like this:

Call in the destroying dark Goddess Izanami. Do not be frightened by her appearance, which is usually not very nice. For those who can embrace her power without fear or loathing, she will gift her help in dangerous situations. Before the magician will either be a map, a drawing of the Islands of Japan, a painting or a model. The magician draws the death Goddess into themselves, and looks over the model/map with the eyes of the Goddess. The magician will be able to 'see' or perceive, in their mind, the imbalance of power in the fate structure that created the inner fate potential for such outer destruction. The magician, with the Goddess' arms within their arms, begins to work in both a physical and visionary way, weaving or unweaving threads, mending broken inner power lines, using utterance to blow or send the sea back, and reaches down to the reactor to scoop up the 'power' of the reactor and eat it.

The magician and the Goddess take that destructive star power into themselves and digest it. The magician, from an outer perspective, seems to be staring at a map or model, while muttering, moving their hands about, blowing on the model and using their eyes to stare down something. In their mind, the magician is superimposing the image of the inner structure of the islands over the outer image of the map or model.

When it is finished, the magician and deity part, and the magician ensures that the deity took all of the inner disaster power with them (i.e. the inner pattern of the radiation or impact). The magician will be ill and weak for a while after the work: their recovery depends largely on their age, health and fitness. This is not work for an ageing magician, one with any chronic illness or medical conditions, or who is run down in general: to do such work would bring death.

1. Methods of working with temples and deities

The map or model itself will have been ritually prepared and linked to the landmass and surrounding sea. When the magician sees the inner pattern of the island and any beings inherent to that landmass, the many layers of that land are brought together before the magician and then worked on by the composite being which is the magician and the Goddess. This is a very powerful way of working and does indeed work. I have used this method in other instances, and what is really curious about it is that when you are invited to work on such a problem, which will happen at some point in your life, you discover other people, most often ones not connected to the situation, were also asked to do the same thing. So when you are called to do such work, and it works, don't pat yourself too readily on the back: chances are a few hundred magicians around the world got a similar call and between you all, you have managed to effect some inner change. That is what being a magician is all about, tending the garden. However, if you are not called, do not act.

And what change can be effected by this work? On an outer level, the results of a few hundred magicians working at top speed can slow certain inner momentums down, which in turn stops that energetic feed to the outer manifestation. So for example, it cannot stop a natural occurrence or a disaster, but slowing down the inner impulse can make it a bit easier for the outer cleaning and regeneration to trigger. What this actually does is ensure that what is happening in the physical world is not leaned on or interfered with by an inner being that may use their energy to perpetuate the disaster so that they can feed off of the results. It can also slow down the 'inner disaster' in general: every outer occurrence has an inner mirror version. The inner version or inner pattern of an event and its subsequent unfolding is what powers the *fate path* of that event and its subsequent unfolding. If the inner pattern can be modified, tuned or brought into harmony, then there is a good chance that the outer disaster will not be as long-term and horrific as it would have been with no magical intervention.

Back to the technique. In stages it would go something like this: link the outer land or person to the image or model. Bring through the deity into yourself, then work on the model or image using vision, breath and hand actions. When you have finished, the deity disengages and returns back over the threshold. The magician turns around, thanks the deity, closes down the doorway and leaves the model or image on the altar with four candles burning around it to effect a boundary. Leave that boundary/flames in place for about an hour or so as the work will continue to happen. After that time, close the candles down and put the image or model in a safe place.

1.8 Visionary movement

There are many ways of moving power about using vision and movement, and one method has a presentation that looks very similar to tai chi. It is a simple but very powerful form of mediation of power from the Inner Worlds to the outer world. Usually this work is unconditional and you have absolutely no idea what it is doing. This 'keeping the magician in the dark' is a very good way of working, because it keeps the abuse of this technique to a minimum.

When called to do this work, the magician opens up the gates either above him or below him, which are the most usual directions this works from, but it can also be used with the four directions. Once the gates are open and power is flowing across the thresholds, then the magician gets to work. Using movement that looks very similar to tai chi, the magician gathers the power from behind him and pulls it through his body using visionary techniques. The power is gathered within and then is directed outward to a specific direction or is woven with arm movements and shifts of balance before being directed by the hands and the mind.

Elements of this technique can be seen in many ancient forms of sacred dance. For example, Bharat Natyam, a form of temple dance from South India, uses the mind combined with action to send power: As is written in the ancient text Abhinaya Darpanam: 'where goes the hand the eye follows: where goes the eye, goes the spirit: where goes the spirit is the heart: where's the heart is the reality of the being.'

In practical terms, this technique is best developed and practised by working with the weather. If a storm comes in, figure out which direction the storm is coming from and work with your back to that direction. Be totally open in your mind and do not try to direct, affect or suppress the storm: let it flow through you and work with it to achieve whatever the consciousness of the storm is trying to achieve.

1. METHODS OF WORKING WITH TEMPLES AND DEITIES

You can then learn to work with the storm which in turn teaches you a lot about the health of the land.

Once you get used to working with the weather this way, then if there is a really dangerous situation, you can work on nudging the direction of the storm (which is a last resort action). The key is the tiniest but focused intention: this has a lot more affect on a storm than brute force. The one thing to never ever do is to try and suppress a storm: to do so could bring death to a lot of people. The aim of this line of work is to get to know how storms work and how they think. With that information, you develop an affinity with the weather which enables you to gain insight into where a storm is going and how powerful it will be, which in turn gives you the information to get out of it path. Most storms are doing a job that is absolutely necessary for the health of the land, and to interfere with that can create a cascade of problems.

The other way that this movement/power technique can be used is to break up power patterns that have become 'looped' and are destructive. This can be a side effect of badly done magic, or magic that is aimed at a person or household for malevolent reasons, or unhealthy patterns that have built up in the land or in a property. All power and magic leaves a trail or thread of energy, and when there is a buildup or aftershock after a magical event, it can begin to loop over and over in a pattern that in turn affects the area and people around it.

If you just wade in to break such a pattern or loop of magic, it can dig in and resist any attempt to break it up. But if you use the method of movement and 'weaving' to echo or copy the pattern, over and over until you have merged with it, then you can break the pattern by suddenly breaking away from the pattern once you had become established with it. This is a very old form of magic and has been used in many ways for both good and bad. Essentially, you use the method of copying and merging with a power pattern, being, or person until you are no longer detectable. Once you and the pattern are one, you take the lead of action and by breaking the action, the original pattern also breaks. It's also a great way to catch horses: follow them, copy them until they forget you are there, then change direction and they will all follow you!

1.9 Summary

Once you have established a working temple, either by moving an ancient one or creating a new one, and you have connected the temple up to inner contacts or deities using doorways, then you are ready to begin the Work. Magical temples are not there to play with: they are working spaces where the magicians unfold their work of service, development and exploration. As an adept, the emphasis on learning should now be over, and the focus should be on engaging everything you have learned to begin to do something useful. In truth you never stop learning, but if you constantly approach the Work with an agenda of learning or self-development, then your work will eventually plateau and go no further. Power only really comes together when there is a good reason, and when it does, the urge to Work will be almost unbearable.

Chapter Two

The magic of the fire/volcanic temple

With the understanding of elemental magic in the early parts of training comes a realization that the powers of these elements can be moulded magically and used with pinpoint accuracy to build powerful magical structures. One of the most prevalent and prolific forms of this elemental building is the Fire Temple. The history of the fire/solar temple reaches back into the far distant past of our humanity and is the most powerful 'formed' expression of the power that streams both from fire and from the sun. In history, the streams of fire magic split into solar temple and Fire Temple, which in its Underworld expression is mainly taken up with volcanic powers, and its overworld expression which is from lightning. But the source power is the same: it just expresses itself differently. The volcanic form of magic is older in terms of power usage, but the solar magic has been the most prolific magical stream through history and has given us numerous strands of solar temples, out of which came the solar kingships.

The majority of expressions of the solar power in the Near and Middle East, Europe and Central America expressed themselves through the male power, hence their association with kingship. But there have been some female expressions of this power, usually in much older traditions i.e. Japan, early Egyptian dynasties, Yemen and Nordic myths. I will deal with the solar lines and overworld lightning lines of magic later, which are completely different realms of magic.

But of the two streams, the volcanic stream is more interesting, more ancient and certainly more powerful to work with. It appears in disguise in British mythology (Vortigern's cave for an example) and is still scattered around the world in various mythological forms, which can be referred to when searching out images from magical working visions. It has survived in magical practice up to the present day, although some groups that use this form of magic have dressed it up and dumbed it down to sell to the masses, which in turn has caused the inner contacts of that work to walk away in disgust. It is a very fragile form of magic in that it is so old, beyond our humanity, that it needs careful handling for its integrity to stay intact. The other possible problem with this stream of work is that the contacts are so ancient that they are not of our humanity, so when they appear in the visions of the magicians working that form of magic, if they are not prepared for what is coming (or they are stupid), they think the contacts are aliens because they are not fully human. This problem happens when people who have natural sight stumble across this work without understanding and don't pause to discover what it is that they are actually seeing.

2.1 The use of volcanic magic

Volcanic power is about forging new lands, melting and transforming, and it is also about the raw power of the planet. It is about the metals within the rock, the releasing of those metals and their powers, and the transforming of those substances into magical tools. So straightaway you can see how powerful and potentially dangerous this form of magic could be in wrong or stupid hands. It could also be very dangerous in the long term if it was in ambitious hands: this power creates, along with solar power, civilizations, temples and kingships. Hence sovereignty is nearly always associated with the sun and the sword (liquid metal drawn from rock, which is the volcanic part of the deal). The volcanic power forges the path, creates the weapons, and intermingles with the sea power to make new life, and the solar power gives it growth, beauty and strength.

But that is the historic picture; what about today's magic? The power of volcanic fire can be drawn upon for a mass of reasons, both in personal use and wider service. The majority of volcanic magical work starts out through visionary work to ensure the right inner contacts, knowledge training and inner flexibility to hold the power safely. Once that training and ability is in place, then the outer expressions can be worked with in ritual and in mediation, and in direct physical action with volcanic sites. The reasons to work with this power are many: for example to rebalance and assist a volcanic site where magic has been used and has caused an imbalance. It can also be worked with to forge powerful magical tools, build temples, and to work unconditionally with the inner contacts and beings connected to the volcanoes in the rebalancing needed after human interference (i.e. bomb tests, etc. and to attempt to temper an impending eruption that poses major risk to living beings. From an inner point of view, this power can also be worked with for building Underworld temples, reaching back to connect with prehuman contacts, and to work with 'dragon' power that is expressing through the land in an unbalanced way and causing problems.

2.2 The path to working with volcanic/fire power

It is very important at the outset of any branch of deep magic that its inner patterns, energies and contacts are connected with and understood. If a magician attempts to work a new form of magic without attending to its inner aspects, then the magic will be flaccid and without strength. This is good in that it takes time and effort to delve into the inner aspects of a realm and people who are silly or selfish in their work don't like to put in much effort to obtain the power their desire. It's a sort of idiot filter in the flows of magical power.

The way to gain the knowledge of the inner patterns and contacts is through vision, and lots of it. Every time someone goes in vision to a specific magical realm, they loosen the binds that hold their consciousness into their bodies, until the magician can flow easily from one realm to another. Once that is achieved, a magician can stand at the foot of a volcano and commune with it in depth, commune with the inner beings that reside in the volcano and draw upon the power of the volcano just by standing there and thinking at it. There are no robes, no waving of wands: it's actually quite boring to watch, but the results can be devastating in their strength.

Once the visions can be accessed properly and enough contact has been made, then the next step is to learn to mediate the power of the volcano into an object, usually a sword. That alone will set off a whole new path of magical work that could last years as one learns to properly wield a sword that carries the fire power of the Underworld. With the knowledge of the sword, ritual workings of volcanic power can become extremely powerful and have to be handled carefully and thoughtfully: it is one of those streams of magic that can destroy the practitioner if it is not handled properly.

Work with the following visions in the sequence in which they are given, and work with each one a few times until the contact is established before moving onto the next one. As with all visionary magic, once you have found a suitable connection with a contact, the vision will take on its own life as you are shown the patterns and structures that are best accessed by you. Always remember: the vision is merely a window of constructed imagination through which the contact can connect and communicate with you. All of the visions in this book are ancient paths that have been used over and over for millennia, so they are well-worn and their inner patterns fully tuned to their frequency. Once the vision is fully established in reality, then you will find it begins to take on a life of its own as you move away from the constructed pattern and connect with what is currently happening in that space.

2.3 Visions of the volcanic temples

These visions are truly ancient and stretch back to a time and power that we associate with the myth of Atlantis. (Dare I say that word without cringing?) The mythical pattern of Atlantis reaches back to an ancient memory of a consciousness and power that drew its strength from volcanic energy and solar power. It comes from a time before 'our' type of humanity existed, but the waves of its magic still wash up on the shores of our world today. The following vision was given to me by an inner contact when I was in a time of great need for this form of power.

Fragments of the priestly workings of this magical path were written into my first novel *Azal: The Retelling of Eve*, which outlines in its later chapters the patterns and methods used in solar and volcanic fire magic of that time. It also highlights the problems of power drunkenness than can scourge a magician when he or she dips their toe into this form of magical work. Once the work is fully connected with, it can give access to a very focused and potentially destructive form of magic that must be used wisely. Thankfully, this magic also has a safety valve in which those who try to use this power for unhealthy ends tend to suddenly shut down as the contact withdraws their bridging. It is heavily dependant upon the contacts for it to work, and once you veer onto a path of self use in a power grab, the contacts withdraw and the work becomes useless twaddle.

The visions are laid out in a specific sequence that gives you the information you need to work with this form of power. It is important to first observe and understand the inner structures of these massive earthly powers before then going onto make contact with the beings that work within these structures.

2.4 Going into the city beneath the waves

Light a candle and with eyes closed, see your flame burning within you quietly. See your inner flame and the flame of the candle merge, feel the peacefulness that surrounds the flame and within that peace, see the flame grow bigger before you, filling you with warmth and peace. With the intention of wanting to reach out for knowledge regarding the temple of volcanic fire, you walk into the flame and feel its gentle warmth flow over you. The flame falls down into the Underworld, passing through the building, rock and earth, and you follow.

You fall and fall through earth and rocks, falling and falling through darkness and silence. As you fall, your memory of the surface world falls away and you fall in a still peace, as if you have always been falling. You fall through caverns, crystal caves, dark stones and also just darkness, where you cannot see anything around you. Eventually you fall on soft sand, finding yourself in a dark cave with no features. A light touch upon your shoulder makes you jump and a being that you cannot see properly hands you a kind of boiler suit to put on, a hat for your head and glasses for your eyes. Once you are suitably dressed, you are led to a corner of the cave where there is a small opening in the ground and a rope ladder descends into darkness.

2. THE MAGIC OF THE FIRE/VOLCANIC TEMPLE

You are prompted to go down the rope ladder without explanation, and as you climb onto the ladder you feel a deep fear rise up within you as you begin to climb down. Don't worry about the fear: it is a natural instinctual reaction to the power building around you.

Down and down you climb, climbing through darkness and silence once more. But this time you feel heat all around you, which builds slowly. It is then that you realize your suit is there to protect you from the heat. Down and down you climb until once more you land in a small cave. To one end of the cave is a tunnel out of which shines a dull light. You venture down the tunnel, which emerges out onto a ledge. Below you is a vast ocean floor and you realize that you are under the sea somehow, but the water does not affect you. On the ocean floor is a series of buildings, like an ancient city with step pyramids and beautiful buildings with vast ornate entrances. Many of the roofs are covered in gold, and the city seems to emit its own gentle light.

You dive in and swim down to a building that really draws you. Upon entering the building, you find a stairway that winds around the directions in a square shape as it descends. You walk down the stairs, noticing the murals on the walls as you walk. They seem to be telling a story of history and you stop for a while to look and absorb the story. Once you have seen what you needed to see, something urges you to climb further down the stairwell until you come to a doorway. Placing your hand upon the door, you feel shapes and sigils outlined on the door, magical symbols that protect what lies beyond. As your fingers scan the shapes, you come across one that you recognize and with that recognition, the door quietly swings open.

In the room, which is built of stone and has a stone floor, is a square stone plinth. Looking closer, you realize it is actually a stone cube that is partially set into the floor. It is at that point that you realize that the building, and in fact the whole city, is all straight lines: there are no curves, no archways, no circles. You are drawn to stand upon the stone plinth, your feet upon a square marked out in gold in the centre of the plinth. Standing in silence, you gradually become aware of an immense power beneath the plinth. It is then you realize that the room has the odour of sulphur and that it is hot. Something about the shape of the room catches your attention: it is very harmonious, but strange. The walls work at a specific angle to

2.4. Going into the city beneath the waves

the floor which gives the appearance of a slight tilt, and the more you look at the walls of the room, the more you become aware of lines of energy flowing along the joins of the walls and floor. It begins to feel like you are standing in a massive battery.

The room begins to communicate with you, not as an inner contact or as stored information, but as the shape itself: its lines, corners, and angles all have their own vocabulary, and as you look to understand, you see that the angles, corners and lines all act as conduits for power. Looking up for the first time, you see that the roof rises to a pyramid point, and all the lines of power that are drawing from the source beneath the plinth are being channelled to the tip of the pyramid.

Your attention is drawn back to the plinth, and you are now aware of the fact that what is beneath you is a volcano and that the building, in fact the city, is built around and upon the volcano. The plinth is the epicentre of the building that caps the volcano, and you are standing in the very centre of the top of the volcano. The power flows along the lines of the room and is gathered by the tip of the pyramid which vanishes into a room above, looking at this you realize that you are looking at an externalized form of patterned ritual: the power is flowing around lines, directions and shapes, and it is mediated from one direction (below) to another direction (above).

Your mind struggles to understand, but something deep within you tells you not to fight, but to let the power flow around and within you, and that will bring its own form of understanding. The humanity that built this place is very different from our own, and you must let your body translate for you rather than your mind. With that understanding, you lie down on the plinth. We are a humanity of imagination and emotion. The humanity that built this place is a humanity of logic and mathematical structure. You cannot use your imagination as a doorway to understand this temple: you must allow the ancient common memory within your blood to remember in its own way. Lie down and close your eyes. Let the power of the volcano flow all around you. You fall deeper and deeper into a still place. You drift without time, without thought, without movement. You drift into a deepness that stills everything within you. All is silent, all is peaceful.

2. The magic of the fire/volcanic temple

In that state, you feel a deep shift in your consciousness, like an ancient remembering. It triggers a déjà vu feeling, a sense of aura, of remote memory and of scents and sounds that skirt the edge of your mind. From that deep place, a sound wells up in your lungs, a deep resonant sound that breaks through a barrier and is released through your vocal cords. It is a deep harmonic sound that you did not know your body was capable of making. The room begins to vibrate from the sound, like a bell, and the lines and angles become bright with power. A force of immense strength, the life force of the volcano explodes out from beneath the plinth and flows through the room and your body. The nerves and muscles in your body twitch with the connection of power, and the endocrine glands in your brain suddenly feel bright and full of power. The power in the room flows up to the pyramid tip, but the power flowing through your body seems to have no focal point and flows around and around your nervous system.

Just when you think you are going to explode with the power, some memory somewhere deep in your brain knows what to do and you stand, extend your arms into a direction and shout a deep loud sound. The power gathers together in the spine in the area of the back of your neck and then shoots out through your arms and through your voice. The power levels are immense and you have no control over what is happening. The sound and lines of power from your body shoot through the wall of the building and vanish. You collapse down onto the plinth as the power leaves you. You must now get back on your feet and leave this place so that you can observe what has just happened.

Leaving the room and climbing up the stairs, as you look at the paintings on the wall, you see a painting that depicts something similar to what has just happened to you. The power of the voice in the painting shows the immense destruction of a city by an explosion of wind and fire: it looks like a nuclear bomb has gone off. As you emerge out of the building and begin to swim back to the ledge, looking back, you see a line of destruction through the old city, a line that is from your call of destruction. What you did has flattened the inner patterns of the buildings in a straight line in the direction in which you held your arms out.

2.4. Going into the city beneath the waves

You swim back up to the ledge, pondering on the implications of this ancient form of mediated volcanic power. Certain things in ancient and biblical history begin to make more sense to you now: they were racial memories of this ancient and very destructive power. As you climb your way back to the surface, more and more things regarding patterns, shape, power, numbers, geometry, etc. begin to make sense in terms of magic, power and how the universe works. The closer you get to the surface, climbing your way up through the cracks in the rocks and on rope ladders, the more the information that had been stored for millennia in your genes surfaces to your conscious mind. As you emerge from the Underworld and sit back in front of the flame, you look around using your inner vision and notice for the first time, faint lines of power following shapes around you, and power flowing through the nerves in your body. You remember all that has happened, and you particularly remember how the power of the volcano was funnelled through the shapes and through your body. You sit for a moment in silence and stillness before opening your eyes and blowing out the candle.

★ ★ ★

That vision introduces you to the form and pattern that underlies the volcanic form of fire magic that flows through human consciousness. Once you have learned that form, it opens up the structure for you to find other and probably safer ways to work with that power. It has been used over the millennia in the construction and destruction of cities in the early era of city building. The same form of power emerges in various ancient civilizations around the world that built city states, and I was curious about why the same power emerged in almost the same way at locations that were not connected (that we are aware of). It took me years to figure out that while they did not have direct contact, the knowledge in the Library of our humanity can be accessed by those who know how to do so. The early city and temple builders were masters of occult knowledge and as such were able to access ancient wisdoms, just as we do now.

That construction and destruction power has little use in today's world, as it can be so devastating. It is akin to a nuclear bomb, and thankfully our consciousness is slowly moving away from the use of

2. The magic of the fire/volcanic temple

such power. It can be used, with great care and restraint, in temple building, but I feel there are much safer ways to do it. However, even though it is a power that is falling into oblivion, it is important, like all histories, to study it, learn about it, and put it in context. It is important to know about it so that you can deal with it safely when you come across it. It is a power, though, that corrupts very easily and becomes dangerous very quickly. If you know how it works and what it does, then you can also gain the knowledge of how to dismantle it and make it safe. Such work is part of the work of an adept, and such things will be put in your path to deal with.

2.5 The cave in the centre of the world that links all volcanoes

This is a very curious, interesting and powerful place that is manifest in the inner world but has no real direct expression in the outer world that we currently know about. The way it manifests in the Underworld is as a cave at the centre of the planet. Now we know that such a place could not possibly exist in the manifest world, but its expression to us tells us that it is deep in the Underworld, is very old, and is a place where the power of mountains comes together.

When I first started to work with this place, a fellow occultist remarked that it was very similar to a place that occultist Bill Grey had found when he was working with mountains in the Himalayas.

Magically, it is a place where mountains and volcanoes at opposite sides of the planet can be worked with simultaneously. I also found, after a short while of working in this space, that fault lines can also be worked with from here. I used to work in this place if there had been underground bomb testing that had caused blockages, or if magical pathways through the Underworld had been blocked by an earthquake. It is important to note at this point that outer occurrences like earthquakes, volcanoes and the like affect pathways through the Underworld and can have a knock-on effect through the Inner Worlds magically. Sometimes it is fine and is just change, but at other times it can block ancient pathways which then isolate inner beings and cut off access to Underworld temples and places.

2.5. The cave in the centre of the world that links all volcanoes

I once came across a really good and interesting example of this many years ago when I lived in a place called Pointe Reyes in California. It is a small peninsular that juts out into the Pacific Ocean, and it is a wild and beautiful place. As I was driving home one night from San Francisco, I noticed a large boulder that I always pass which lay on the boundary of the peninsular. An inner contact loudly announced, as I was driving and singing along to Bally Sagoo, that I had a job to do with that boulder and it was time that I got to it! The day after, I did 'get to it' and went in vision to the boulder and asked it if it needed help. A being appeared beside the boulder and told me the boulder was fine, thank you very much. I was confused. Normally when I get a contact like that, it really means that there is a problem. I told the being this. "Oh," said the being, "it will be to do with *them*," he said, as he pointed to the ground under the boulder. "Them?" I asked? "Listen," the being said. I sat very quietly, and sure enough I heard a very faint call for help.

I went under the boulder in vision and found a small tunnel that I could just about fit through. A short way into the tunnel I came across an abyss: a crack in the ground that seemed to go on forever. On the other side, peering out of the gloom, were a motley collection of faery men, all dressed in Tudor sailors' clothing. I was fascinated! What the hell where these English faery men doing in California? They shouted at me to get them out, but as I looked around I could not see anything that would create a bridge across the abyss. It was short enough for me to straddle, though, as I was a lot bigger than them. Eventually I laid across the abyss and they climbed over my back and up out from beneath the boulder.

As I scrambled out they were running towards the sea, waving and shouting thank you. As I went home, all I could think was what a bloody weird experience it had been. I could not figure for the life of me how the hell they had got there. I guessed that they had been trapped by an earthquake: that area sits right by the San Andreas fault line. A few days later, when I tentatively told a friend what had happened, she replied that they probably came from one of the ships. Ships? I asked? Yes, she replied. Drake's Bay, which was close by, was called Drake's bay because Sir Francis Drake got stuck there for a winter while they repaired a badly damaged ship. The light bulbs went on...an English Tudor Ship, close by in dock for a few months.

2. THE MAGIC OF THE FIRE/VOLCANIC TEMPLE

The faery men must have been on board the ship, left to explore the powerful land where they had stopped, and got trapped by an earthquake, unable to get back to their ship, which sailed off without them.

I then began to fret about what would happen to them once they got to the bay and found no ship, and that hundreds of years had passed. I went down to Drake's Bay, but did not find them. I never saw them again.

So, back to the cave. The following vision can be used to work on fault lines, volcanoes, and mountains. It can be a part of service to the land to keep this place in balance, and it can be worked with to relieve tension in fault lines and volcanoes when the tension has been caused by magical interference or underground bomb testing. If the volcanic or fault line activity is natural, then no matter what the consequences of an earthquake or volcano on humanity, you must not use magic to stop natural disasters. It is very tempting, particularly when there is the possibility of many deaths, but unless you have an inner prompt from a contact, it is important not to interfere in the Earth's natural processes. What may be bad for us may be very necessary for the planet's health and survival, and we have already, as a species, done enough damage by manipulating the environment to suit ourselves.

Sometimes, though, there is what seems to us to be a natural disaster unfolding and inner contacts will kick us into action to do something, and it is always a matter of understanding that we have an extremely limited ability to 'see' what is going on in the larger picture. If you have strongly established contacts, then they will come to you when work needs doing, whether the disaster is a natural occurrence or not. Here are two examples of such scenarios. The first happened in the middle of a working group session. I was teaching structures to do with the Fire Temple and a contact started to badger me during the sessions. They told me they needed a group to do a job and would we be willing? Of course, me being me, I always agree to a job before actually taking the time to find out what it is.

The contact showed me a desert scenario, and below the surface of the desert was what looked like balls of explosive fire straining at an invisible membrane: it was about to breech, whatever 'it' was. We

2.5. The cave in the centre of the world that links all volcanoes

all set to work and slowly released the pressure on the membrane before guiding the fire power through channels into storage caves, down into tunnels, and mediated some of it out into the air where it could disperse. Some of it needed real heavy containment: it seemed very toxic and was killing everything around it. So between us all, we took it down deep into the earth to the bottom of the Underworld, as far as we could go, and called upon a deep and ancient goddess (a precursor to Sekhmet) to ask her for her help. She ate up the toxic fire power and that was that.

When we came out of the vision we all had light sunburn on our faces and hands, and we all felt like shit. After consuming vast amounts of coffee and chocolate, we sat around discussing what we had just done and what it actually was. I did not recognize the desert where we had worked, and I had no clue about what we had actually just done. But one of the women in the group did know. She recognized the patch of desert and mountain as being in Nevada: it was a particular military underground dump for spent nuclear fuel and decommissioned weapons. This is why I often say that you do not need to go out looking for the work, it will come to you: there is enough damage out there caused by our species to keep you going through multiple lifetimes.

The second example of being guided to work on a natural disaster was when I was living in Tennessee. I had just finished my work for the day at the ballet company and it was the day that I only worked until mid-afternoon. I was very tired after a gruelling week of rehearsals and training sessions, and I was just about dead on my feet. When I got home I went straight to my bedroom and lay on my bed. On my wall bedroom was a six foot icon of the Black Madonna, a goddess contact I was currently working with. Before her were a mat and a candle: I would sit there each day during my working pattern with her, doing what I usually do. As I was laid out on the bed, listening to an old recording on CD of a group of Tibetan monks singing the skeleton dance, a contact made an appearance and demanded that I sit before the icon. With the chants still going, I had to light the candle and go into the Void. I was unsure about doing a vision, as my baby grandson was asleep in the next room, and I am always wary about doing visions so close to children from my

2. THE MAGIC OF THE FIRE/VOLCANIC TEMPLE

family: they tend to come along for the ride. But the contact almost screamed at me to get going.

I went into the Void, the chants still going in the background, and I felt a huge amount of pressure build up before me. It was bearing down upon me and I had to very gently and carefully push it to one side. I had no idea what it was or what I was doing. It was a tremendous strain, and I was relieved when it finally faded. I was brought out of vision and the contact told me I could now go and rest (gee, thanks). I fell into a deep sleep for two hours and awoke suddenly as though someone had shouted at me. I staggered into the kitchen where my daughter was cooking and my grandson was gurgling away in his chair. I still had no idea what the hell had happened, until I plopped down in front of the TV and watched the news.

A storm front had been building all day, and as it moved towards Nashville it had been spitting out tornadoes. One had been on a path straight towards us, but it had veered away at the last moment and trashed a small neighbourhood a few miles away. It shook me up when I realized the implications of a tornado hitting our tiny little house, with no shelter and a baby inside: it did not bear thinking about. So you can see how contacts will sometimes step in to get you to work. I had no idea if the storm was natural or not: the point is that I did not work on it intentionally, but was guided into unconditional work by an inner being.

2.6   The vision of the cave

Light a candle and with your eyes closed, see your flame burning within you quietly. See your inner flame and the flame of the candle merge, feel the peacefulness that surrounds the flame and within that peace, see the flame grow bigger before you, filling you with warmth and peace. With the intention of wanting to reach out for knowledge regarding the temple of volcanic fire, walk into the flame and feel its gentle warmth flow over you. The flame falls down into the Underworld, passing through the building, rock and earth, and you follow.

2.6. The vision of the cave

You fall and fall through earth and rocks, falling and falling through darkness and silence. As you fall, your memory of the surface world falls away, and you fall in a still peace, as if you have always been falling. You fall through caverns, crystal caves, dark stones and also just darkness, where you cannot see anything around you. As you fall, you can hear water rushing by and splashing, but you cannot see anything in the deep darkness. You fall and fall until eventually you feel you are just falling through space, with nothing around you, no rocks, no earth, just falling and falling. Eventually you slow down and fall into a spherical cave with a sandy floor.

The cave has its own glow to it and you look around in wonder at its beauty. It is a very large round cave with many holes in the walls that vanish off up and down into darkness. You realize that you have just fallen down one of those holes. The walls of the cave are littered with sparkling outcrops of various types of semiprecious crystal stones, veins of precious metals and clumps of very primitive fungi. The cave is warm and damp, with a faintly strange odour that you recognize but cannot exactly remember. You begin to explore the cave, which is pretty large and has a strange quality in that it is spherical and there seems to be an odd gravity. You can keep walking around the cave and realize that you are walking the full circle of the sphere: you are walking the full surface of the inside of a sphere without falling off the roof.

Once that novelty has worn off, you begin to explore the holes, some of which are large and some of which are small. As you put your hand into the holes, which are actually the entrances small narrow tunnels, you discover that the inside of each tunnel is smooth and shiny: it is quartz rock that has been smoothed out through millions of years of being touched and stroked. Placing your hand on the quartz, you stop the urge to stroke the smooth rock and you quietly become aware of a pulse in the rock. The pulse from the quartz flows up the tunnel which passes through the earth and emerges on the surface of the land, either at a fault line, a mountain or a volcano.

It takes a while for your inner sensitivity to catch up with the huge number of vibrations that flow in and out of this cave, but as you go from hole to hole, you realize that the holes each have their own pulse frequency, and each hole is unique. To experiment, you place one hand in one hole and another hand in another. You

2. The Magic of the Fire/Volcanic Temple

feel the two different pulses flowing into your body from the two different holes. The vibrations begin to harmonize and communicate within your body and the pulses flow from one hole to the other in a deep, pulsed conversation. As they flow through you, you can see in your mind's eye the sources of the two vibrations: two mountains on different continents. The mountains commune with each other in a flow of natural power that brings balance to them both.

You are prompted to break the connection from some deep instinctive place and you are drawn to another hole in which you place your hand. The pulse in this hole seems to be blocked, and is echoing back into the cave rather than flowing out into the world. You push your hand up into the hole to feel where the blockage is, but it is too far up for you to reach. Instead, something tells you to blow hard up the tunnel, which you do. The pressure builds up from you blowing until you feel it give way, and your breath vanishes up to the surface. You feel a deep rumble and shift before the pulse of the quartz reestablishes itself up this tunnel. Stepping back, you realize that your breath has just released an energetic blockage that had caused a pressure buildup in a fault line, and the land had shifted to loosen itself once more.

So now that you know how this space works, you can come here again when this type of work is needed. But for now it is time to leave. You have to ascend slowly from this deep place, and you climb back into the hole that you fell out of. If you cannot remember which one it was, walk around them until you feel one that is very familiar: that one leads to the land upon which you live. You climb back up the tunnel, feeling the pulse as you go and feeling the land around you, the rocks, the pressure, the fault lines, the mountains, rocks, hills and springs: the roots of all of these land expressions are in these tunnels. You climb and climb, taking care not to dislodge anything, and taking note of the different scents, rock types and occasional beings who sleep in the land as you climb. If you pass one of these beings, pass slowly and quietly so as not to wake them. As you emerge out into the light of the surface world, you remember the candle that is before you and you sit quietly, contemplating the flame as you remember what you have just seen and experienced. When you are ready, you put out the flame.

★ ★ ★

That vision can become part of an adept's service to the land upon which they live, and can be used to work with natural earth expressions like earthquakes, volcanoes etc. But it can also be used on a landmass that is supposed to be open and breathing but is trapped by concrete, buildings, etc. There are a variety of ways to work with this power and the best way to find out all of its applications is to work with it and discover its power and function as you go. It can be used to relieve power in a volcano: rather than block the volcano, you can release the pent-up power so that the eruption dissipates faster and with less damaging consequences.

2.7 The contact of the sword maker

This part of the Volcanic Fire Temple is fascinating, beautiful and very strange: it is probably the oldest part of the inner structure and most certainly the part that is prehuman in its inner construction. I am not sure of its full use magically speaking but I am sure that it has far more applications than I have discovered, though it does seem to be slowly drifting out of our conscious realm. The inner pattern of the temple and its beings/contacts usually survive for millennia beyond the outer construct, and when its builder's civilization has fallen into the dust the inner pattern still ticks away, slowly fading over thousands and thousands of years until it is finally barely a whisper. This contact is fading, but is still strong enough to be reached in vision and worked with.

This contact works deep within the volcano and works with metals, their powers and their transformation. The contact itself appears in a prehuman lizard/raptor-man style form, very similar to beings that appeared in Babylonian bas-reliefs. The image itself is not a major revelation to occultists: this form of being seems to pop up all over the place in its work with humanity. When I first started to work with this contact he taught me a lot about swords: the power that can flow into a sword, how to weave beings and powers into swords, but most important of all, how not to use a magical sword. He also taught me about the power lines of magic that flow from the volcanic temple that is in the previous vision, and how to break those lines and safely dispose of them. So that has been most of my experience with this contact. I do not know if that is all that he does: I'm sure he works in a wider field, but I do not have that wider experience with him. For those of you who feel a great calling to this part of the work, I am sure that over the years of your work the mysteries of this place will unfold far beyond what I have seen.

2.8 The work with swords

Once of the most interesting things I learned from this contact was a way to work with magical swords I had not previously come across and it was a way that seemed to make a great deal of sense. Instead of putting power or a being into the sword as a consecration/mediation that then stays for the life of the sword, this contact places into the physical sword an immensely powerful line of fire power that works on the job in hand and is then taken back out again. At the beginning of the work, the magician visits this contact, has the power placed in the sword, goes off, does their job and then immediately comes back and has the power taken back out of the sword and placed back into the volcano. This has two major benefits: the first is that it allows a much greater power than normally would be mediated to be put into the sword for the job at hand, and the second benefit is that the magician is not tempted to misuse the power over time. By having the sword empowered for only one job, there is no possibility of what can usually happen with magical swords, and that is that the magician, upon realizing how much power a magical sword can wield, begins to use it to solidify their own power base.

The other nastier temptation is to then use the sword to wipe out one's enemies. One who attacks with a magical sword will reap destruction down upon their whole society (the magical wisdom hidden in the Arthurian Mysteries) because the power in the sword is enough to destroy a whole nation. The magical sword, when used to defend a nation, is not wielded in battle, but is held forth as a being in its own right.

> Then they heard Cadwr Earl of Cornwall being summoned, and saw him rise with Arthur's sword in his hand, with a design of two chimeras on the golden hilt:

when the sword was unsheathed what was seen from the mouths of the two chimeras was like two flames of fire, so dreadful that it was not easy for anyone to look. At that the host settled and the commotion subsided, and the earl returned to his tent.

— *The Mabinogion*, translated by Jeffrey Gantz

The power that can be wielded through this method of working is not to be handled lightly or without serious reason (usually a life or death situation for a person, being or nation). It is tremendously destructive both to whoever is on the receiving end of the magic and to the person wielding it. Remember the basics: you mediate your own magic, so it flows through you before it goes anywhere else. People forget this over and over, and then are shocked when they get hit on the rebound (which takes its own time, but does happen eventually). If the power is used to cut magical binds, spells, curses, to bring about justice and balance, or to guard a land, nation or area in dire circumstances, then such power will also do the same to the handler.

2.9 The vision of the sword maker

This vision takes you to the contact and introduces you to his power. I have purposely not included how the sword is worked with: you will have to figure that one out for yourself. But if you truly need that power in your work, then the contact will guide you.

Light a candle and with eyes closed, see your flame burning within you quietly. See your inner flame and the flame of the candle merge, feel the peacefulness that surrounds the flame and within that peace, see the flame grow bigger before you, filling you with warmth and peace. With the intention of wanting to reach out for knowledge regarding the temple of volcanic fire, you walk into the flame and feel its gentle warmth flow over you. The flame falls down into the Underworld, passing through the building, rock and earth, and you follow.

You fall and fall through earth and rocks, falling and falling through darkness and silence. As you fall, your memory of the surface

2. THE MAGIC OF THE FIRE/VOLCANIC TEMPLE

world falls away and you fall in a still peace, as if you have always been falling. You fall through caverns, crystal caves, dark stones and also just darkness, where you cannot see anything around you. You fall and fall through darkness, the scents of the earth, the rocks and underground rivers swirl around you as you fall. You can hear the roar of an underground river that you pass by as you fall, and the deeper you go into the belly of the earth, the more you begin to smell the scent of sulphur. You begin to slow down and eventually you fall on soft sand, finding yourself in a dark cave that is hot and sulphurous. There are loud noises all around you, and as your eyes adjust to the dark you start to see a gentle glow coming from a tunnel carved out of the rock.

You begin to walk towards the tunnel. All around the entrance are carved into the stone strange frightening faces and many intricate patterns made out of squares, triangles and straight lines. The walls of the tunnel are lined with gold and punctuated with crystals of many different colours. The crystals reflect light in all directions, and steam swirls around your feet. The deeper you go into the tunnel towards the orange glow, the hotter you become, until it becomes uncomfortable. Just when you think you cannot take the heat anymore, the tunnel opens out into an underground cavern where part of the floor falls away to expose the bubbling lava of a volcanic pool. You get as close as you can comfortably stand to the pool, and you call using the sound that you learned in the earlier vision.

Once you have called a couple of times, a being emerges from a hidden crevice and walks towards you. The being appears as part reptile, part human, with a spinal ruff of feathers down their back. Its movements are very calm, quiet and considered as they walk slowly towards you, summing you up as they walk. The being does not speak to you, but gestures for you to watch the volcanic pool. The being opens its mouth wide and calls a strange noise that echoes around the cavern and seems to create vibration that is picked up and amplified by the stones and crystals that are in the walls around the cavern. The vibration seems to get into your teeth and your bones, until your whole body is vibrating at the same frequency as the being's call.

The being motions for you to step back, and you do just in time to see an enormous dinosaur-looking being raise its head out of the

2.9. The vision of the sword maker

pool. Its head is so large that it fills the pool, and its eye is the same size as your body. It turns its head to look at you, and it gazes deep into your eyes. The gaze and the sound seem to change something about your cellular makeup: the vibrations and power of the gaze reach deep into your past, the past that flows through your blood, and awakens something. This ancient being is of a power that is rarely experienced in the world anymore, and just standing in the presence of this volcanic giant is enough to effect change, which is what power does: it changes things. The being that is the contact that guards the cavern places a hand upon your shoulder and then seems to fiddle about with your throat and the back of your head. This gives you a headache, but you begin to hear and see differently. You can see the lines of metal that run through the cavern, and the flow of power that pulses through the veins of both these ancient beings.

It is enough that you all have looked at each other and had contact: now it is time to leave, but it is advisable to visit this place and to learn from the contact both about the powers and beings of this realm, and also how to work with precious metals and the tools forged from them.

The contact being guides you out of the cavern and shows you an ancient stairway that reaches all the way up to the surface world. They back away and leave you to find your way back up to your own realm. You are guided by the memory of the candle flame that you are seated before, and that memory pulls you back up as you climb and climb. Just when you think you cannot climb another step, a small tunnel with a dim light to your right beckons you, and you climb up through the earth and rocks to find yourself emerging back in the room where you started.

You sit before the candle flame, pondering on what you have just experienced, and when you are ready, you blow out the candle.

★ ★ ★

When that contact is worked with in terms of working with a magical sword, the being in the pool is the one that takes the sword and puts power into it. You can imagine the intensity of the power that can flow from this magical work. But before you rush off to

2. THE MAGIC OF THE FIRE/VOLCANIC TEMPLE

conquer the world with a magical sword, there are a couple of things you should know.

Firstly, the sword has to be virgin: the blade must not have drawn blood, which of course is a given in all magical work with swords. It must also have been magically stripped of all influence, salted and grounded. Once the power has been in it, that is all it can be used for. Once you return the power, the sword has no other use than to wait until you go back to this place to repower the sword. It is not a ritual sword and cannot be used in ritual, not even when the power is not in it. It has become a vessel for that power only and will have no other use at all. Put it away with a guardian to watch over it, and never ever let anyone fool around with it, swing it around, or point it at anyone. The reason for this is that once it has been used, even though the power has been taken out, remnants can remain, and even the smallest remnant of that power can kill or damage someone.

The second thing you should know is that while the sword carries the power, you carry the sword, which means you have to hold the burden of that level of power in your body while you do the work. It is a vast amount of power to have to carry, even for a short piece of work, and the effect on the body can be considerable. The effects may not be obvious straightaway as the inner impact, although felt while you are working, will not fully manifest for days or even a week or so after the work. Then you can be hit so badly that it may make you very ill. Hence this work is only done when it really needs to be done. The load cannot be shared with anyone, and there is no way of dodging around this aspect of working with this implement in this way. The holder bears a terrible burden and is this is expressed as part of the Mystery to do with the Sword of the Land and the Sacrificial Kingship. This whole aspect of work is the source of the dragon/volcanic/fire/sword/king myths, mysteries and stories. The king or queen would be a keeper of the sword and would empower it in times of peril. The sword would be carried across the land and its dragon power released to do what was necessary to bring about peace and stability. The king or queen would carry the terrible burden of the sword on behalf of their people and the land, and woe betide any who misused it: it would destroy them.

The sort of work that would warrant the use of this sword spans a variety of situations from slicing through complex Kabbalistic bindings and serious death curses, occult attacks upon a nation, war, drought that is caused by magic (natural disasters should never be interfered with: they are usually bringing balance for the land) the dealing with large ancient beings who are disturbing volcanoes and waking them up (usually woken up by magic) any very large fire being that is wreaking havoc and nothing else has worked. This method of working with the sword is a last resort, as it holds a power similar in its destructive capacity to a nuclear bomb.

In general, any of the fire/volcanic magic is volatile and dangerous just by its own nature. But you must also take into account that this form of magic has been misused over and over again throughout time to quench various thirsts for power and revenge. It is a raw, vicious power that can wield great good in the right hands and terrible destruction in the wrong hands. The safety valve is the amount of physical burden such work puts upon the human body: this burden tends to put off most people with bad intent, but there are occasional madmen or women who will do anything to further their agenda. Hence the care with intention, the care with guardians, and the willingness to work unconditionally, working blind with inner contacts as simply a cog in a very large wheel.

Chapter Three

The power and magic of utterance, sound and sigil

One of the purposes of magic in humanity, particularly in the West, is upholding the structure that allows civilization to exist. In this day and age, we often wax lyrical about how wonderful it would be to get back to a simpler time, to live closer to nature and away from civilization. But there has to be a balance. I would bet that very few people reading this would know how to forage properly, hunt and kill their food, keep warm in winter, protect themselves and live on the edge of existence all the time. It's a very romantic idea, but in reality nature is harsh, vicious and deadly in northern climates. Without the basic structure of civilization, we would dwindle as a species very quickly.

That does not mean that we turn our backs on the sacred land and the feral powers of nature, it means that we must keep a balance between the two and treat both with extreme respect for we need both to survive. As magicians or priests, there is a great deal of work to be done to uphold both nature and the magical inner structure of civilization and society. The ritual structures of society are basically the patterns of magic as expressed through the civilizations of the Near East and are the foundations of magic today.

In this chapter we will look at the direct patterns that influence civilization and society. The most prominent, the earliest and the most enduring pattern of magic in this field is concerned with the power of recitation. From myths, stories and songs, recited wisdoms, the inner power of utterance, to the calling upon the deities, and the language structure that gives rise to invocation, sigils, and sacred alphabets: the use of words/breath creates magic of all kinds. Language in magic is used to bind, release, move power, bring a

3. THE POWER AND MAGIC OF UTTERANCE, SOUND AND SIGIL

being in or send a being away: the scope of this magic is endless and its potential is beyond our meagre understanding.

We will start by looking at the relationship between the angelic thresholds of this power, the mediators and the manifestations. It takes all three for this power to flow into the manifest world and our job, as humans, is that of mediator. The most externalized form of this role as mediator is found in the monotheistic religions. The angel speaks wisdoms to the man, the man listens, the man goes and tells others. It has become a well known and well trodden (and often misused) path for the utterance of Divinity. But there is one problem with that scenario (hence the problems, wars, etc.) and that is that the utterance of Divinity is not about understanding what is said, or wise words or platitudes; it is about power.

The power of utterance is a way that humanity can cope with the manifestation for the frequency of sound and vibration that is Divine Being: i.e. the words don't *mean* something, they *are* something. The wisdoms became lost somewhere along the way and by the time we got to Jesus and Mohammed, that power had become a series of teachings and pronouncements. They knew that to utter something in the name of God was special, but the true magical implications and applications were lost by that time as the Near East became mired in tribal wars, Roman wars and general mayhem.

The mediation of the Divine Utterance of the Universal Power is the same as mediating the patterns of the Metatron cube, for instance, or the putting of a deity into an object: you are taking a power with no face or form and putting it into something that will be able to function in the outer world. The sounds *do* things. The words *are* things, and putting the sounds and words together *creates* things. And then you have the layers: words that *are* things but also *mean* things, so you can utter a sentence which will *mean* X, but the sounds themselves have their own power and will *do* Y. You can see the potential for powerful magic and also for dangerous misuse. A lot of quite vicious magic developed over the centuries through the use of word and sound, and gradually the constructive use faded into the mush of reciting religious or magical texts in the feeble hope of it doing something, anything.

This magical use of language, both spoken and written, is virtually everywhere where there is a magical or religious interface with beings that move beyond ancestors and land beings. But for this chapter I will concentrate on the languages, scripts and ciphers of the Near East, because that is what I know best. The techniques in this chapter can be altered to work in any other culture, for example Nordic, Sanskrit etc. All of them have angelic and demonic beings that work through the languages: they are known by different names, but the powers are the same.

The following visions take the magician through the whole process of the mediation of the power of utterance, and show the various octaves that this power can operate through, from the depths of creation to the magical interweave between a name and a power. Although the visions expressed here are situated loosely within the Judaic stream of consciousness, the techniques can be transplanted to be used in any tradition: once you get to a certain level of power and depth in any tradition, the interfaces and methods are more or less the same, because you are working with what is actually there, not a construct.

Once the visionary work has been done, the inner contacts have been established and the magician's body has adjusted to the impact of being close to such power, then the mediation can be transferred into ritual so that the power is worked with in a visionary ritual format. That is when it is at its most powerful, and care must be taken always when working at such level.

A word of caution: if you work at any real depth with this power it changes how your voice works (sometimes literally). You become able to create patterns of power using your voice without intention or thought. Most very powerful magic flows from the magician unhindered by conscious control: you have to be very careful at all times about how you use your voice, your words and your meanings. Once a magician has mediated power at this depth, they never switch off: you become a twenty-four hour open door for power, and what you say in anger can have devastating consequences. Hence this work is laborious and time-consuming: it takes years to climb the ladder safely.

3. THE POWER AND MAGIC OF UTTERANCE, SOUND AND SIGIL

The first vision is the deepest. It puts you in the position of the mediator of creation with the archangel and angel at your back as filters. Creation started with a sound: all flows forth from that sound and all becomes that sound. You become the Pontiff, the bridge; and as the power of utterance passes through you, it changes you forever. From that point on, when you work with utterance, sigils or speech, that power will trigger at some level and begin a magical process within you. You will truly understand the power of utterance, which covers magical speech, sigils, alphabets and the power of the wind.

You cannot control what passes through you, though, and trying to work at this depth with an agenda is sheer stupidity. To even think of doing so is madness. You are messing with the powers of all creation and while is it an honour for you to be allowed access to this event, and to passively participate, it is a crime above all crimes to try and filter, control or shape it. Why? Because we are an incredibly stupid, dense and shortsighted species. Not only would what we create be pathetically primitive, taking control of this power to form it would put you in the driving seat, hence all the power will descend upon you and will not be upheld by anything else. As a passive mediator you get to experience it, but you are not responsible for it: you are not upholding it. Once you take the reins it is all yours, and if you think for a minute...a manifest human body in relation to the whole of creation...well...it's a bit on the heavy side, even if you go to the gym.

There are a few who have got access at this depth and have tried to control, weave and form the power as it leaves them: they attempted to harness the power of Divinity and they just ended up leaving a mess on the floor. So for any pentacle-festooned black-clad 'magician' reading this with the keys of Solomon on the table beside them, be warned: piss around with this stuff and you will become a flurry of epithelial cells blowing gently in the wind...

The reason for working with this vision, and it is the only reason, is to change you deeply inside so that your body and soul touches base with the constant act of utterance/creation at the edge of existence. Creation was not a one-off Big Bang event: it is happening all the time. In the Inner Worlds there is no time, only action and reaction. The constant existence of the act of creation and destruction ensures that the world keeps turning, babies keep being born, and new species keep constantly flowing out of the Void. Because we are bound by substance and time, we view events and expressions of power as one-off happenings in a linear sequence in time. This is not the case. All lives are happening at once, all deaths are happening at once, the single act of creation is constantly happening, and you will always have credit card debt. Okay, back to work...

As usual, light a candle and sit quietly in a place where you will not be disturbed. Once you have become used to working with this power and are not easily distracted, then go out onto a hill and do this vision using the wind/air instead of a flame as an elemental gate. That would mean being aware of the wind and then joining with the wind in communion with that element.

3.1 Vision: the mediation of sound at the edge of the Abyss

With eyes closed, be aware of the candle flame before you and of the flame that burns deep within you. As you look at the candle flame you are drawn to the flame and find yourself stepping into the fire and bathing in its cleansing flame. The flames do not burn: they are the brightness of the spirit of Divine Being. The deeper you walk into the flame, the more regenerated you feel, and your inner flame grows in strength and vitality. You pass through the flame and find yourself deep in the Void, the place where there is no sound, no time, no movement. In stillness, your outer structure falls away and you find yourself drifting without form, flowing with the wind that blows in and out of this place as it carries power into manifestation. You are blown with the wind out of the Void and out into the Inner Desert. The wind swirls the sand and out of the swirling sand walk two angels of great height: their long hair, which trails behind them, swirls with the sand and their legs vanish deep into the earth.

One of them reaches out and grabs you by the hair. The moment they touch you, brightness throws sparks out of your skin and hair, like static. They pull you through the Inner Desert to the edge of the Abyss and make you stand, looking over the Abyss to the mists on the other side. The mists seem to be moving, like a very slow tornado,

3. THE POWER AND MAGIC OF UTTERANCE, SOUND AND SIGIL

and a very deep, almost inaudible growl is coming from the moving mists. The hair on the back of your neck begins to stand up and your whole body screams with fear, but the angel holds onto you so that you cannot run. You are committed.

The mists seem to get deeper and thicker, with resonant rumbles and groans adding to the noise. The ground begins to shake, and rocks begin to fall into the Abyss. Beings who were sleeping deep in the sand begin to wake and emerge, and the sand itself begins to give off a very bright intense light. At this point the angel turns you around and puts a hand over your eyes. A massive archangelic being emerges out of the Abyss: a being of indescribable proportions that is so powerful his light is trapped deep within him, like a black hole. His frequency is a very high vibration of sound in opposition to the deep growl of Divine Being across the Abyss. The Archangel puts his head back and screams at a really high pitch, which hurts your head and makes the sand grains vibrate very fast. Different tones begin to sound, and when they lock together in a specific harmony, the power of Divine Being, the deep growl in the mists is pulled through the dark centre of the Archangel and is combined with the high-pitched scream.

This combination of frequencies is transformed in the body of the Archangel and becomes the Wind of Many Sounds. The Archangel leans forward and tries, ever so gently, to blow the Wind across the Inner Desert. The Angel of the Desert, who is standing behind you, shielding you and protecting you, filters the wind through their backs and blows a fragment of it through them and into the back of your neck. The Wind builds up within you like a great pressure. You feel as if your lungs are going to burst from the pressure, and your heart begins to race as it fights to cope with the power.

Just when you think you are going to black out, the angel pulls back your head by the hair and screams in your ear: "Recite! Recite the name of That which Cannot Be Named! Recite! Recite!" Your mouth works as you try to form words that your brain does not understand. Your mind struggles to convert the Wind/Name into something you recognize, but it cannot make sense of it. The angel tugs tighter on your hair and screams once more at you. Your body takes over, your mouth opens, and out comes a series of strange

3.1. Vision: the mediation of sound at the edge of the Abyss

sounds: they jumble and compete as the different frequencies try to escape.

What you cannot see, because you are shielded from the knowledge at a deep visual level, is the words blowing like little whirls in the sand, joining with the sand and taking form. They become animals, trees, birds, rocks, and people. Every living thing upon the Earth, within the Earth and above the Earth forms from the mediated sound of Power. Lines of existence, fate and manifestation emerge out of the sand like a giant skeleton, which the creations are drawn to and finally merge with. The two combined become the world that we know, with all the lives, deaths, and patterns of action embedded within them.

The last breath issues out from you and you collapse onto the sand, the angel still holding your hair. The Archangel vanishes back into the Abyss and the mists of Divine Being are still once more. You find that you cannot stand, you cannot speak and your lungs are on fire. The angel picks you up by the hair so that your eyes are level with his eyes. He looks into you and the look bores right through you, like a beam of light searching for something. The light hits parts of you that were damaged by the mediation and it fills those parts with light to allow them to heal. The angel then picks you up and strides off down the Inner Desert with you, taking you towards the threshold of your life, beyond your birth, through your childhood and up to present day. He walks and walks through every aspect of your life while he carries you, and although you are cradled, exhausted in the arms of the angel, you recognize points in your life where you subconsciously picked up on this angel striding through your life with your soul cradled in his arms, maybe in dreams, or daydreams, or just a weird feeling of being held and protected. You had a strange déjà vu sense that you were not alone and that you were protected at certain points in your life, and now you begin to remember those points in time and realize what it actually was that you were picking up on.

The angel arrives at the time where you are sat before the candle flame and he gently puts you down in your body as it sits before the flame. He rubs balm in your eyes. He pours oil down your throat. He blows gently into your lungs and he takes out plugs that he had put in your ears to protect you when you were not looking. The angel

3. THE POWER AND MAGIC OF UTTERANCE, SOUND AND SIGIL

blesses you with the blessing of life and death, and then vanishes into the flame.

You look at the flame for a while, remembering what happened and feeling your body and soul settle together again. When you are ready, you blow out the candle flame. As you blow, you feel a power on your breath and that power directs the flame into another world. You realize that you have been changed, and that your breath has the power of utterance and all the responsibility that goes with it.

★ ★ ★

3.2 Utterance in the temple

The next octave down the scale in that work is to mediate the Utterance in the temple. This again is a very old working that was a major part of temples of the Near and Middle East and laid the ground for religions that worked with language, sound and shape. As an aside, the most degenerate form of that expression is a religion of the book. By the time the 'Book' had taken hold, the power was already gone and the rot had set in.

This working method steps down the power of the Abyss work and forms it into a shell or Qelippah. This second octave, the first step down from the raw power expression of Divinity, is what the Kabbalistic Qliphoth really is (instead of a load of large-breasted demons in drag). This Qelippah is a form that allows the Divine Power of Utterance to express itself in the manifest world, and it creates a barrier between the magician and the true depth of the Divine Utterance. Because this second octave puts shape and face to the frequencies, it is inherently unbalanced, as any boundary or restriction on unformed power will compress it and contract it, therefore making a shape.

All the different octaves of this work are repetitions of the original act at the edge of the Abyss, but each octave is more formed, more detailed, more approachable, and therefore more corruptible. If a temple is working with this power, then the original act at the edge of the Abyss must be regularly done in the inner sanctum to ensure that the outer, more manifest Qelippah do not degenerate and

3.2. Utterance in the temple

contract too much. If the perpetual utterance at the Abyss ceases, the Qelippah becomes more and more contracted, which makes it more degenerate and therefore more dangerous. Both ends of the seesaw must always be in action: if one ceases to express power, so does the other one. If you have the outer manifestation without the balancing octave, the Qelippah becomes a true shell: an empty husk devoid of power which then is usually hijacked by inner parasites who move in, dress up in the shell, and tell hapless magicians that they are demons and have great powers. Those magicians who lack proper inner experience take the Qelippah at face value and a truly degenerate, parasitical and powerless relationship begins.

The second octave is the utterance of magical form into the temple. This level of utterance creates the interface for Divinity to manifest through a pattern which can be interacted with by humanity, which is basically what magic is: an interface between Divinity and Man. This magical interface can either be worked with in its genuine form, which is technique, or it can be moulded into a religious structure. In the magical form, the utterance creates vibration patterns that become vessels and bridges for power. The magician learns to work with the patterns and the beings that uphold those patterns, and through that interaction they learn to work with the inner powers of all the worlds to effect change.

If it is stepped down into a religious structure then it must be further contained, and gates are created, along with gatekeepers, to separate man from Divinity. The religious structure and its hierarchy then act as mediators between the people and Divinity: it simply becomes a more heavily filtered pathway. And the more filters a path has, the more chance there is for corruption and power grabbing. The filters are the Qliphoth which, if allowed to become empty husks, are filled once more with parasites who protect themselves and their food source by dogmas which are designed to keep the feeding station under control. It is easy to see how religions and magical paths start as amazing, wonderful, powerful paths, but under the bad management of humans quickly become degenerate, dogmatic, parasitical means of control.

Back to the second octave. The following vision is the technique for plugging into and working with the second octave in a magical temple setting. It can be used to establish a temple, strengthen a

3. The power and magic of utterance, sound and sigil

temple or to open the gates for a flood of new and fresh work. If you are working in a traditional lodge or temple organization, then this vision, if done fairly regularly in sequence to the first octave, will keep the lodge and its magicians healthy, and the work will trot along at a strong and clear pace. Doing each of the first two octaves twice a year if you are a lodge or order will be enough. For an individual adept I would recommend the first two octaves done once a year at key points in the year. These two lay the path, keep the door open and keep you, the vessel, clean and balanced for the Work.

3.3 The vision of utterance in the temple

With eyes closed, be aware of the candle flame before you and of the flame that burns deep within you. As you look at the candle flame you are drawn to the flame and find yourself stepping into the fire and bathing in its cleansing flame. The flames do not burn: they are the brightness of the spirit of Divine Being. The deeper you walk into the flame the more regenerated you feel and your inner flame grows in strength and vitality. You pass through the flame and find yourself deep in the Void, the place where there is no sound, no time, no movement. In stillness, your outer structure falls away and you find yourself drifting without form, flowing with the wind that blows in and out of this place as it carries power into manifestation. You are blown with the wind out of the Void and find yourself standing on a threshold between two worlds. Behind you is an immense swirling tornado that has eyes and wings, and before you is the temple in the outer world where you work.

You are standing upon a threshold, and the threshold is an angelic being who is the gatekeeper between the Paradise of balanced power and the outside manifest world of imperfection. You can feel the being move and flex beneath your feet, and you feel its power seeping through the soles of your feet, travelling up your spine. The feeling becomes more intense and you realize that the being is slowly climbing into your body to be a co-mediator with you. The being slowly inches its way up your spinal column and into your brain. It stretches out in your body and begins to merge with your nervous system. Your vision changes and you begin to see how this being sees and feel what it feels. Before you are lines of light and dark, the

3.3. The vision of utterance in the temple

air moves thickly like an intense swirling fog and the space seems to be constantly fragmenting and reforming. The space is devoid of sound and it feels like you are observing a vacuum.

You become aware of the tornado raging behind you and also aware that you can see all around you. The tornado has many eyes, many wings and is getting denser and denser with each second. Your attention to the tornado pulls it closer to you and a power begins to build up that leans against you, pushing at your back. You struggle to stand upright and the being within you grips the floor with what feels like talons gripping a perch. Your head and neck begin to arch down with your chin reaching for your chest, as if coiling a spring ready for action. Suddenly the angel snaps back your head and the tornado behind you flows through you at high speed.

As it hits your vocal cords, strange sounds come out of your mouth and form into shapes. The shapes settle themselves around the room and embed themselves into the walls and objects in the room. Lines of power come out and weave patterns of light and dark across the space of the room and the patterns connect up with the shapes. The wind stops, the angel suddenly withdraws back through your feet into the threshold and all is still. You stand for a moment, on the threshold between two worlds, your eyes seeing the room but the residue of angelic sight showing you the patterns and shapes of the power that was uttered.

Something pushes you forward and you fall into the room, the patterns vanishing. You stand before the central flame, feeling the fullness and profound stillness of the room. Everything has changed energetically, everything is alive, everything is charged ready for work.

Leaving the candle going, you open your eyes and sit for a moment drinking in the peace. When you are ready, leave the room, leaving the candle going, and let the space readjust to the magical patterns that have just been impressed into the fabric of the building. You will feel when it is time to put out the flame and have the sense of simply sending the flame into the Inner Worlds rather than putting it out as you blow.

⋆ ⋆ ⋆

3. THE POWER AND MAGIC OF UTTERANCE, SOUND AND SIGIL

This vision enlivens the room and embeds specific lines of power that are to do with the magic of utterance, language, alphabets and sigils. You would use this vision in your magical space/temple if you were about to embark upon a term of service that deals with anything from magical writing, to working with sigils to constructing ritual. It will ensure the full powers of recitation are with you and will also open the gates wide to the depths of that power. It can also produce impressive puffs of wind outside as you come out, which really looks good and always causes a stir...

The next stage down from that vision, the next octave, is to work with sigils and sacred writing. Essentially, it is the same working again, just at a different frequency, a different octave, and the power is stepped down once more. In our power-crazed world, the idea of stepping down power to work magically, as opposed to raising power, often causes a flurry of discontent among those who wish to impress. But if the power is too high, then it cannot fully manifest in the outer world. The more manifest something is, the less powerful it is: the density of physical manifestation limits the amount of power that can express through that density. When the power that is attempting to manifest is air/utterance, then its most exteriorized form is an alphabet or sigils.

The sigil form that expresses out of this power is not the type of sigils that are beings and powers within themselves, but is a lesser version, power-wise, that consists of marks, names and 'brands' that carry the power of intention or identification with them. This work would be done to either create a new magical alphabet, create individual sigils for specific jobs, or to invigorate one that already exists. When you are creating a new alphabet, you are reaching for that power of utterance and aiming it through a filter that forms the vibrations into sounds and then images. If you try to create a magical alphabet or sigils without the inner utterance, then the image of the letter has no power within itself and it becomes an empty shell that other 'vibrations' or sounds that are a part of parasitical consciousness can step in.

The vision that we will work with takes us to an ancient Underworld goddess from whom many magical scripts and alphabets have emerged. It is a step down from the power of Utterance at the edge of the Abyss, as this is a formed, specific goddess, and she has her own place (the Underworld) whereas Divine utterance at the edge of the Abyss is Divinity without form, the most powerful form we can get to without ceasing to be. This is the difference between Divinity and deity.

It is important to understand that such an alphabet does not give rise to a language that can be used in sacred communication: that is a totally different kettle of fish. This way of working allows you understanding of the sound of certain places and beings and gives you the key to lettering those sounds onto places and things to help connect up beings to places and events. The same goes with sigils: when they are created this way, they provide a key to a specific place, event or person and allow a connection to form and grow. The actual creation and mediation of this form of alphabet is done in vision, with some physical action of writing, but then after that, the utterance and letterings are used in ritual action and intent.

The next vision takes us to the creation of a sigil or string of sigils that are to be used for a specific purpose: it is the creation of working tools that then become a major part of the ritual structure within the temple. It works with and builds upon the previous vision, and once you have worked with all octaves of this form, you will find that they begin to intermingle as you work, and echoes of one will awaken the thresholds of the others. Once the sigils or letters have settled within you, they will begin to unlock and emerge as you work. This can be done as a seated vision or can be done standing at an altar.

For this work the altar must be in the east with nothing upon it but a candle flame. Anything on the altar could potentially act as a filter for the power as it is mediated, fragmenting or even blocking the sigils. Besides, working at this magical level you should have got past the whole New Age product display altar.

3.4 The vision for the creation of magical sigils

Light the candle flame in the east and stand with eyes closed. See the candle flame with your inner vision and see beyond the candle flame two gates that slowly swing open to reveal a pathway of columns that vanish into mist. See yourself stepping through the candle flame

3. THE POWER AND MAGIC OF UTTERANCE, SOUND AND SIGIL

and walking through the mist with the columns on either side of you. Some of the gaps between the columns have fire pedestals, which throw off a faint light, and others are in complete darkness. The effect is light, dark, light, dark, as you walk through the mist, and you find yourself becoming slightly disorientated.

As you walk and try to penetrate the mist to see what is up ahead, you hear a strange breathing, almost like panting, echoing out of the mist, and the volume of sound would suggest something very large and animal-like ahead of you. Treading carefully, the side fire pedestals vanish and you are plunged into a misty darkness with just the sound of panting to guide you. Suddenly, two priests holding up flaming torches appear before you and challenge you. One looks into your eyes and seems to delve deep into your soul, and the other demands to see the soles of your feet. When they are happy with what they have found, they turn and stand beside you and each puts a hand upon your shoulder. They walk you forward and as they walk you get the feeling that they are holding you not to support you but to stop you running away from something.

As you walk further into the mist and get closer to the panting noise, the hair on the back of your neck starts to stand up in alarm. All of your inner warning bells are ringing and your heart begins to beat faster and faster. The two priests throw you to the ground before what looks like a large boulder. The boulder moves. It is then you realize that the boulder is alive and is actually the tip of a big toe. You look up and see that you are at the feet of a gigantic being that is seated and all you can see are the legs up to the knees.

The giant being slowly lowers a hand for you to step onto which immediately raises you up into the clouds and brings you level with the eye of a great black being who is part human, part lioness. The scent of lions is all around you and she stares at you, unblinking as you stand like a speck of dust before her. She looks at you, and then looks into you as if checking that you are a suitable container. She asks you what you want and why you want it. You reply that you are a magician and wish to work with sigils within the temple as magical tools.

When she is sure of what she sees, she begins to whisper, her lips barely moving. As she whispers, she releases one of her claws and cuts a line between your eyes, which immediately begins to bleed. The blood gets in your eyes, making it difficult to see, and the heat rising from the hand of this great Goddess is making you burn with its power. The cut begins to really sting and distract you, and just as you are about to put your hand to the cut, the whispering noise of the Goddess gets louder and louder. Her pitch changes from high to low and to areas of sound that you cannot hear. You brush the blood from your eyes so that you can see what it is she is doing.

Her lips move and out of them, formed by the sound, come shapes. The shapes travel towards you and push themselves into the cut in your forehead and drive themselves through your skull and into your brain. You can feel the shapes trying to find a place to nestle in your head. The pain is unbelievable. More and more shapes appear and push themselves into your head, and you feel your body begin to buckle under the pressure. She breathes the last shape, which pushes its way into your mouth rather than into the cut upon your brow. The she blows on you, hard. Her breath, which smells heavily of lions, blows at you like a hurricane and takes your breath away. She then stands up and begins to climb with you in her teeth until she reaches a cavern that is too small to take her, a cavern which also has a crack of light at the other end of it. She motions for you to go through that crack and then pushes you. You walk towards the crack and the light, and as you get to the opening in the rock a priest steps out to greet you. He looks at the blood on your forehead and is instantly aware of what has just happened to you. He takes your hand and guides you carefully over rocks and down tunnels until you emerge out of the side of one of the columns in the mist.

He walks with you and explains to you that you now hold a magical alphabet that is directly linked to her power, which is the power of death, medicine, war and healing: the powers of destruction and regeneration. The priest tells you that he will act as an inner contact with you so that you can learn to work with this alphabet properly. He shows you his right hand, which has a strange mark upon the palm. Remember that mark: it can be used to call him or to have his power work with you on a project. You will be instantly recognizable to any priest or priestess of this line by the mark upon your forehead, and all inner beings will recognize you as touched by Her.

3. THE POWER AND MAGIC OF UTTERANCE, SOUND AND SIGIL

You walk back towards the threshold of your world, leaving the mists and columns behind. Stepping over the threshold, you return to your seat and look at the flame with your inner vision. You reach out, take the flame in the palm of your hand and put it into yourself. Once the inner flame is safe within you, you blow out the outer flame. Immediately go and draw the sigil of the priest that was on his palm, and once you have done that, go and sleep: the knowledge and keys that have been placed within you need to settle and reemerge into your conscious mind.

★ ★ ★

The first thing to notice about that vision is that is it getting closer in its action and presentation to our world and the Underworld which upholds it. The second thing to notice is that the sigils or alphabet are not shown to you, but put within you to unravel in their own time. If they were put in the head, which is this goddess' favourite method of transfer, then you are likely to have blinding headaches for a while until the sigils settle and make their way out of you. If they were put into your mouth or you have to eat them, which is a delivery method favoured by angelic beings, then you will probably have the shits for weeks. Anything that has to do with angels and scripts, books, scrolls or sigils is usually processed by the body through the alimentary canal, and anything from Underworld Goddesses tends to be in the head. If you are working with the sheer power of Divine utterance, then it tends to pass through the lungs and the back of the neck, and those two areas usually take a hit.

I have yet to come across any script or sigil transfer by a male deity, so I have no idea how such a transfer would affect the body. It is pointless trying to theorize over what would happen, or even to theorize over why the body has such a reaction in general: it just is what it is, and your time is much better spent getting on with your work. When working with inner dynamics, things happen in the most bizarre ways for the most bizarre reasons. If you try to push for an intellectual dissection of what happened and why, then you will lose the ability to flow with the power. If you just let it be, the reasoning will emerge into your mind in its own time. Once that has happened, then you will be falling over texts that explain or describe the process in minute detail. Everything in the Inner Worlds has its own time.

So you are full of sigils and shapes. What next? Well, there is no magic button to press that will release them; they will come out in their own good time, usually when you come across something that one of the sigils is ready to connect to, or when the alphabet is needed to be put to work, and then it will all tumble out. This can be a quick or a slow process, and there is no way to tell which way it will go. If you can divorce yourself from your mind, then you may be able to automatic-write them, except then they will be out of context and you will not know what they mean. It is much better to wait and let them come out as they need to. Once it is all out and working, you will find it was worth the wait and the work. Usually the first one comes along pretty quickly and will initially emerge as a familiar sound that you connect to a being or place, swiftly followed by a sigil. You will then start to see the sigil everywhere you go... it is the Inner Worlds' way of saying, 'did ya get that?'

The rest will tumble out as and when. Just make sure that you write each sigil down with a note about what it is connected to. If you do not, you will remember the sound and what it is connected to, but you will not remember the sigil. This is an inner defence mechanism for the sacred sigil: it will not stay in people's heads independently.

3.5 Working with the sacred sigils and alphabet

Once you have mediated the script and it is completely manifest, what then?

Sigils and scripts that are mediated like this have a number of uses. Some work as calling cards or keys to unlock areas and open gateways. They also mark areas, in the Abyss for example, they can change the power of whatever they are linked to, and they can connect up people, places and objects. They can also act like an open phone line to a particular being or realm. So once the sigils/letters are within you, it is like you have a font folder within you and as beings/deities connect with you, they will see that you are storing sigils of utterance and they

3. The Power and Magic of Utterance, Sound and Sigil

will show you which ones can be used to call them or connect with them.

If you are working with a being as a guardian, for example, then rather than having the being there all the time, which is not really necessary unless they are guarding an Inner Temple, they can leave behind their imprint, which is a sound. That sound is converted to the sigil within you and drawn out. The sigil is like a window to that being and if someone opens a box, comes into a room, picks up a magical tool etc., it will ring the doorbell and call the being: the sigil is like the eyes or ears of the being. So it would be marked where it was needed. To mediate the mark, you would first listen to the sound of the being in vision, and while in vision, with pen in hand, let the being guide your hand to draw the sigil. This takes practice, as you have to block your mind out from wanting to control the shape, but at the same time, the mind needs to be present to allow the being to mediate properly. Automatic writing is a step beyond this, as such a method is truly passive. The mediation of sigils has a wee bit more control and interaction than that.

If you practice this a few times with a being and a place or deity, when you hit the right one, you will begin to see it everywhere. Just don't allow the Goetia sigils to creep into your mind: often ancient magical sigils look nothing like them. Once you have had a couple of successes and you have got your confidence, then you will find it much easier. The other method of getting the sigils out from deep within you is to again tune into the sound of the being or place and hold that sound in your mind. Ask to be guided to the shape of that sound and you will begin to see a sigil everywhere you go, and it will be the only one you can draw. These are placed upon containers, upon Inner Temple doors and outer temple doors, or over the entrance of Abyss tunnels where you are working and want the beings to find you, or you to find them.

3.6 Sacred alphabet

Bringing through a proper sacred alphabet is a lifetime's work but a very fruitful project. To do this, you would have to work with the whirlwind in the depths of the Inner Temple and bring it out one sound at a time. The sound will manifest its own shape within your mind and the angelic contacts will again point it out to you so that you recognize it. One way to do it that will take less than a lifetime is to focus on producing eighteen sounds. Each time you work with the angelic threshold and the Whirlwind in the Depths (which is an archangelic being) a vibration and shape is put within you to carry out. Doing it one at a time is much easier upon the body and is less likely to kill you. It also gives you time to work in depth with each sound to find out what it does, what its power is, and how you work with it. Once all eighteen are out, then you can begin to work on stringing them together in a power weave to create interfaces for Divine Power to flow through. You will find that some work together well and others do not. You will also find that when you get certain sounds together in a pattern, things happen, doors open and power flows in. Certain harmonies will open certain worlds up and other harmonies will destroy. Certain harmonies will connect with certain star alignments and others will tune in with the movement of the planet. Some harmonies will have mathematical expressions that mirror events, and so on.

A word of warning. Do not get trapped in the dead end of attributes, tables, qualities, note expressions, and other such patterns. Don't burn the midnight oil trying to match things up: you will find all sorts of connections with the letters/sounds, but that is immaterial: what is more important is to work with them and actually do something. It is a common trap that many people fall into.

Lastly, the most externalized of all expressions of Utterance is poetry and song. Going into the Inner Worlds and standing before the wind that blows out of the east, allowing that wind to blow through you and then translating that wind through your emotions is a very powerful form of expression, and is the basis for speech in a contacted ritual. You basically plug yourself in during a vision and let that power flow through you as you then begin to write. What comes out is literally the voice of the gods.

At the beginning of this section, I mentioned that when you work in depth with the power of Utterance, it changes you at a deep level. It changes your voice, often literally, it changes the power that flows through your voice, and it empowers your words magically. Because of this, you must be very careful how you use your voice and be very

3. THE POWER AND MAGIC OF UTTERANCE, SOUND AND SIGIL

aware that your words hold power. A casual off-the-cuff wish can turn deadly as a directed chant. The wind flows through you and with you: choose wisely how you work with that wind.

Chapter Four

The magical dynamics of fate

The life events of every living being seemingly follow a pattern of fate that can, to an extent, be predicted. Going back in history we have many myths and stories about powers/women who were responsible for fate, for example the Moirae in Greece and the Norns in the North: immortals who weave the pattern of life and death for every man and woman. Some religions, for example the many religions of India, accept a passive role in the path of fate and do not attempt to challenge or change their current and potential life path. Is that valid? I don't think so.

There are many events that happen in a magician's life and many of these events will put you into a collision course with Fate. I use the name Fate to identify a power that that flows through the life of every living thing and is the junction point for the patterns of life events and death. I see Fate not as a deity but as a hive angelic pattern that interfaces and filters power as it manifests. There are certain realms and visions that you can use as a magician to gain a deeper understanding of this power and of how it is relevant to your work and the work of a group or lodge.

The first step in understanding a fraction of this dynamic, which is almost incomprehensible to us, is to gain the understanding that time does not exist everywhere: it is simply a part of us in our manifest state on a planet that turns. Once you step out of the body in a visionary aspect, there is no time. It is very important to gain that understanding, and to also grasp that time, once you step away and observe it, is all happening at once. It is not a linear event that goes from A to B. it is a complex pattern that just 'is' and it can be moved away from or moved into. Hence in vision you can go back and forward in time so long as you have detached yourself in vision from your body.

4. THE MAGICAL DYNAMICS OF FATE

When you cross the Abyss and stand looking back over it at the Inner Desert which is the foundation for the world, you will see all the events of life all happening at once: it is like a large, complex spider web with many weavers and powers shooting back and forth. The interweaving and interlocking combinations and crossings of paths is fascinating and almost beyond our comprehension. We cannot work with the whole picture, which is far too much for our brains to take in, but we can observe a tiny fraction of the process at work, which can help us understand the process better.

Fate is not like a storybook where it is all mapped out at the beginning and can never be changed. Upon birth the child has an array of paths leading from them that they can walk down. Each path has an echo of the others, and some hold more power than others. The actions and choices of the child decide which route they will take, and as the child becomes an adult their paths lessen as more and more choices are made. Sometimes a choice will open up a new set of paths, and each path will have an echo of the others...often very silly unimportant echoes, like having the same names, same places, etc.

The magician becomes involved when those paths are cut across by powerful magic designed to destroy, shut down, bind or kill a person. One could argue that such a crossing of paths is part of their fate, which it very well could be. But if a person's fate has been cursed to the death, then I see no problem in stepping in and removing the magical curse or binding. They will never be able to go back to their original fate path, but they can pick up the threads and open up new possibilities.

The other instance where a magician and the work of fate crosses paths is in the event of a magician being consecrated (not initiation, which is different). This immediately wipes a large chunk of their path and creates a new one. Not everything is wiped, but a lot is overlaid by the communal fate of the consecrated line. Often one spends a large portion of one's life after consecration cleaning up paths and unbinding them. Most lines of priesthood and magic have a lot of degeneracy: curses and bindings within the line that need dealing with. You do what is put in front of you to clean things up. Don't bother getting the idea that you can filter the whole line: you will be given a fraction to deal with and that will be plenty.

So back to the machinations of fate. Let's look at the process from the inside out. Fate begins with the fate of the planet and that is echoed through the fate of every living being. The octaves are interwoven and are virtually impossible to separate out. Starting with the deepest and most powerful expression of fate, we have to go up into the stars. Fate is filtered by the archangelic beings that are the interfaces of the stars and planets. The call for a new life comes from an act of lovemaking and the echoes of the ancestral blood that lies deep in the earth repeat this call: it is amplified by the call of the bloodline to ensure the call reaches as far into the stars as possible. This is an octave of the action of conception that reaches up the Abyss in search of a being for manifestation through a bloodline.

When the call goes up, it sets off a harmony between the angelic beings and the ancestral echoes: they weave with sound to create an interface that a soul can manifest through. Once that weave is complete, a soul is called out of the Void and falls through the interface into manifestation. The following vision looks at this process in more depth and gives the observer an idea of the deepest octave of this work, which in turn will give a worker a better understanding of the more superficial presentations of bridging life.

It will allow you to observe the inner dynamics of the coming together of the fates: just don't be tempted to interfere. This is not a created or psychologized vision: the minute you attempt to interfere, you will be pulled into the soul's orbit and you will have a hell of a job getting out of it. There are fragments of this vision scattered among a variety of ancient texts, including the Old Testament, and once you have worked with this aspect of visionary magic you will begin to notice it in many different ancient and religious texts. Like everything else, the Mysteries hide themselves until you are able to recognize them. It is not a very practical vision in that it is simply used for observations, but once you have worked with it and experienced it, when you come to work within a temple structure around the issue of fate, it will give you are a far wider perspective on how the ritual practices work and why. I do think it is important, wherever possible, to have a full inner understanding of the processes of magic and how the work originally forms itself.

4. The Magical Dynamics of Fate

4.1 Vision of the conception of a soul out in the stars

Light a candle and look into the candle flame for a moment. When you are still, close your eyes and see the candle flame with your inner vision. As you look at the candle flame, it grows bigger and bigger until it takes up all the space before you. When you can see nothing but candle flame, step into the flame in your inner vision and bathe in its power. The flames do not burn you, they cleanse and energize you ready for the work that is about to happen.

As you stand in the flames, you see through them to a beautiful nothing: a space of peace and stillness. You are drawn to this place and you step out of the flame and into the Void: a place with no time, no space and no movement. You feel like you have come home: this is the place where all power comes from and all power goes to: all existence issues forth from this place, and you feel the potential all around you, yet there is nothing here. You spread out in the nothing, aware that you have no boundaries, no restrictions, no lives, no anything: you just 'are' in this place, you are complete. The stiller you get, the more complete you feel, and the less bound by time, shape or manifestation. You move around in the nothing and you become aware that the nothing is in everything that exists, and therefore because you are within the nothing, you are within all things. You feel as you pass through trees, creatures, stones, buildings and you feel as you swirl around time, as though you are turning in water.

As you drift in the nothing, a call echoes through the Void and you drift towards the sound. You find yourself pulled out of the nothing and out in the stars, surrounded by space, power and planets. Each of the stars and planets seems to be breathing and calling, like a choir coming together. Within each star you see the eyes, movement and consciousness of beings coming together. As you watch the stars and planets slowly parade in their orbits and listen to their songs, you become aware of a deeper, more 'earthy' sound, like a deep horn coming from the depths of the planet. As you shift your focus, you become aware of a cacophony of sounds issuing out from the Underworld: the voice of the ancient ancestors. Those whose blood lies in the land call out to the stars to grant them a new generation

4.1. Vision of the conception of a soul out in the stars

in the line of ancestors, and the deep echoes of time mix with the song of the stars to create a whole intricate pattern of sound.

A funnel of wind, a bit like a tornado, appears in the space between the earth and the stars, and it reaches down to the earth and up into the stars. The wind sucks in the sounds and turns the sounds, creating a vortex. The sound and movement draw you in to look closer. Its beauty fascinates you, and the sounds that come together are the most beautiful thing you have ever heard. It touches some deep and ancient memory within you, and the emotion that spills out from you overwhelms you and you begin to weep. Your tears gravitate to the funnel and mix with other echoes of emotions that are woven into the wind. You draw closer still, feeling the power of the funnel and the sounds, a deep instinct within you drawing you ever closer. A hand grasps you from the back and stops you tipping into the funnel, holding you back so that you can observe without being sucked in.

At that moment a bright light flows past you and into the funnel. It drops at high speed to the earth, like a shooting star, vanishing into the clouds of the planet. A soul has just passed you on its journey into life, and if you were stood at the edge of the Abyss, it would have fallen past you on its way into manifestation.

The shooting star left a trail of threads behind it, some linked to the stars and some floating around as if looking for a place to take root. Out of the darkness between the planets, beings that can be barely seen, almost like shadows, pick up the threads and begin weaving. They connect the stars to the earth, and link in the trailing threads to create a beautiful complex pattern. Their fingers work and weave in total focus, and as sections seem to be completed, the weave lights up with a bright glow and harmonic sounds like vibrating strings fill the space all around you. One of the shadow beings offers you a thread to hold, just for a second, so that you can experience the feel of the weave. The minute the thread hits your hands, a terrible weight descends upon you and everything suddenly seems heavy and dark and complicated. You feel a rush of conflicting emotions, images rush past your vision as if you were watching life sequences, but the thing that hits you the most is the sense of darkness and density: you are feeling the full weight of manifestation while you are not within your own body: the reality of the struggle of life hits you full on.

4. The Magical Dynamics of Fate

Something pushes you forward and you find yourself stepping forward into the Void once more. The stillness and silence rush into greet you and once more you are drifting in a place of no time, no space, and no movement. You stay a while, allowing what you have just experienced to unfold itself within you, and here, in this stillness, you remember something hidden deep in the depths of your memory: the feeling of the wind, the sounds of the ancestral call, and songs of the stars. You have experienced this before and your body recognizes it. With that realization, you step forward out of the Void, back into the room where you first started. You sit before the candle flame and focus upon the light of life within the flame. Reaching out, you cup the light in your hand and place it within the flame that burns deep within you. You feel its peace. You feel the Divine presence within the flame. You open your eyes and when you are ready, blow out the candle flame.

★ ★ ★

That vision is the deepest expression of fate that you can experience as a human, and once it is within your experience, when you come to work with the outer more manifest patterns of fate, the experience of the deepest form keeps the more surface work in perspective. It also reminds you of the sacredness of the pattern of fate. Understanding the deep inner movement of power that manifests as paths of fate helps you to understand that the surface details of an individual's life fate pattern are not about events but about harmonics: the life path is like a song that guides you back to the stars.

4.2 Chess and the Inner Temple

The two main temples I have come across that seem to be heavily involved in fate patterns are temples that I call the Sea Temple and the Fire Temple. Both are templates that underpin many ancient religious temple structures, and both can be worked with in depth. The Sea Temple is basically an inner construct of a magical structure that operates from the deep consciousness of the sea and mediates the tides of life, genetics and the weather. Most ancient temples that are connected to the oceans or seas, to Neptune, Oceanus and Tethys or Nammu, etc. are more formed expressions of the Sea Temple, and you can reach the more skeletal generic power of the Sea Temple by going through the more formed versions with a specific intent to go deeper. Every elemental deep temple has outer, more formed expressions that can be used as access points.

The Fire Temple is the same: it is an inner structure that acts as a template for outer manifest temples around the world that deal with deities of fire and volcanoes. Such temples have manifested around the world and some are still functioning. Again, the deep echoes of magic flow from the archetypal temple out into the world through various religious and magical structures.

Fate is a theme common to both temples, and whereas the Sea Temple is concerned with genetics, i.e. bloodlines and species, the Fire Temple is more focused upon souls and bringing through specific beings and people. If you put the two together you have a massive inrush of power that was used in ancient times to bring through priest-kings and priesthood queens.

To view this process up close, we will visit a Fire Temple to observe the manifestation of fate lines through the temple and how that temple dealt with it. The following vision will be recognized by those who have studied certain ancient mythologies and classical myths. The vision is not taken from those myths, however; rather the myths echo what is to be found in the Inner Mysteries of that temple, and what you will observe is one of the Mysteries in action.

4.3 The board game

Light a candle and look into the candle flame for a moment. When you are still, close your eyes and see the candle flame with your inner vision. As you look at the candle flame, it grows bigger and bigger until it takes up all the space before you. When you can see nothing but candle flame, step into the flame in your inner vision and bathe in its power. The flames do not burn you, they cleanse and energize you ready for the work that is about to happen.

As you stand in the flames, you see through them to a beautiful nothing: a space of peace and stillness. You are drawn to this place

4. The Magical Dynamics of Fate

and you step out of the flame and into the Void: a place with no time, no space, no movement. You feel like you have come home: this is the place where all power comes from and all power goes to: all existence issues forth from this place, and you feel the potential all around you; yet there is nothing there. You spread out in the nothing, aware that you have no boundaries, no restrictions, no lives, no anything: you just 'are' in this place, you are complete. The stiller you get, the more complete you feel and the less bound by time, shape or manifestation. You move around in the nothing and you become aware that the nothing is in everything that exists, and therefore because you are within the nothing, you are within all things.

You remember your task to seek out the Fire Temple and with that intention you step out of the Void and find yourself in the Inner Desert. You appear in the middle of the Inner Desert, with the River of Death in the distance to your left and the Abyss in the distance to your right. You set off walking towards the Abyss and as you get closer to the Abyss, a wind whips up the sand and blows you into the far right of the Inner Desert, near the temples at the edge of the Abyss. You are blown to the steps of one Inner Temple, to a large white step pyramid with a box structure upon the top which is decorated with gold. You begin your ascent up some steps that lead up the centre of the pyramid and enter the structure halfway up. You wander through tunnels that meander around and intersect other tunnels. The walls are decorated with complex story images, all of them decorated with gold and precious stones. Eventually the tunnel opens out into an inner sanctum which is a large white circular room with a gap in the roof through which shines a beam of sunlight. On the floor is a mosaic of a man with the face of the sun and the beam of sunshine is illuminating it. In the centre of the room is a cube block of white stone with an oil flame burning upon it. The floor is also decorated with lions, faces and lots of intricate gold patterns and you can see that the beam of light tracks an arc around the altar in the centre. Around the edges of the room are elaborate chairs decorated in gold, and each one has a sigil upon it.

You hear voices in the distance and you walk across the room to the doorway on the other side and peer through. The temple seems to open out beyond this sanctum and you realize that you entered the temple via the inner back door that leads to the Inner Desert of

4.3. The board game

the Tree of Life. Beyond you, through the door, is a vast hallway with columns that reach high up above you. In between the columns are vast statues of deities with altars before them and plumes of incense. Many priests in white robes and with shaven heads are milling around and talking. One of the older ones spots you and gestures for you to come near them. It is only at that point that you realize there is a being behind you and the priest recognized the being before they spotted you. You walk over to the priest and all the other priests stop and stare.

The priest gestures for you to follow him into an antechamber and he leads you into a room that partly opens out into a library. The being stands behind you and the man gestures for you to sit. He asks you what you are wanting from the temple and you explain to him that you wish to learn about the fate patterns that are worked with in the temple. You tell him that you have been out in the stars and have watched souls fall into generation, and now you wish to learn about how those patterns of fate play out magically. The man nods and begins to tell you about the function of his temple. He says that one of the functions is to ensure that the land has a sacred god-king who will ensure the balance of the land, that the elements are kind to the humans and that the land and rivers are fertile. He begins to tell you about a time before the temple, when the land would heave with earthquakes, storms would devastate the crops, drought would kill their animals and that some storms would bring terrible illnesses with them that would kill many of the children. They learned to work with different beings and deities to subdue them, but subduing one often mean angering another. Over the many years and generations, they learned to bring the powers together properly, and one man would mediate the power of God to the land, so that his job would be to be the fulcrum of all powers upon the land. To find such a child would be impossible, so they learned to call a soul of power into the world and then structure fate to ensure that the child survived into adulthood and beyond.

The priest gestures for you to follow him, and he gets up and takes you back into the great hall. You cross the full length of the hall and come to a great bronze door. The being that is with you, an angelic being, turns you around to show you the inner power structure of the hall. The being places a hand upon your eyes for you to look

4. THE MAGICAL DYNAMICS OF FATE

through and you see the complexity of power lines spilling out from the inner sanctum which are being woven by the priests into the various deities that are seated between the columns. He then turns you again to the great bronze doors before you and shows you how the power leaves the great hall, adjusted by the deities, and flows out into the world. You step through the great bronze doors and down some white stone steps into a courtyard full of trees and blossoms. Here there are women as well as men, also dressed in white, but they seem to have a much lesser role than the men and are not allowed into the temple proper. This gives you warning that something about the temple structure here is imbalanced: the women have lesser roles as opposed to just different ones of equal respect and power.

They are all gathered around a giant board game that is laid out in the courtyard. The pieces are a collection of very large, strange-looking beings, with the odd one that looks human. The board is completely surrounded by people watching, and there are four players. As you watch the game, you see that it is not a game of war or strategy like chess, but a game of complex interweaves that must be constantly balanced and an equilibrium maintained. The player's job is to ensure that each move stays balanced while achieving its goal. The more successful a player is, the more they play. If they are unsuccessful, they have to leave and another player takes over.

The priest talks to a man who seems to be overseeing the players, and they both look at you. One of them gestures for you to step up to the board. The angelic being that has been shadowing you steps up with you and places both hands upon you to assist you. Together you step to the edge of the board. The overseer tells you to place both feet over the threshold of the board and then stop there until told to move. The moment your feet cross the line, the board vanishes and you are in a strange world of misty images, lines of bright and dark power, spinning cubes, and many complex multidimensional patterns that are constantly changing and reconnecting. The shock of the change makes you waver, and the angel holds tight to your shoulders to steady you. The angel does something to the back of your head and then pokes you in the eye, which really hurts—but when you take your hand away from your watering eye, you realize you can now see the board with one eye and the strange patterns with the other. You are given a short time to adjust as you watch the players moving pieces with one eye and see the resulting changes to the patterns with the other.

You are then invited to step onto the board and choose a piece to work with. You are immediately drawn to a particular piece, and you are told to put your hands upon the piece. The moment your hands touch the piece, you see a whole weave of life patterns parade before you. You see them as they look in different lives, and what they did. You are told to feel the piece and to see if the piece needs to be active or be moved or left alone. At first you are not sure how to tell, but the angel leans upon you, giving you access to his perception. The board beneath your feet tells you by a sense of touch if a piece is in the right place or not. You can feel that the piece you are holding is in the wrong place, and you begin to move it instinctively to where you feel it belongs. Your right eye watches as all the patterns change. Shapes vanish and new ones appear, some lines are broken, others are connected, and then suddenly there is a sharp movement and the whole pattern clicks into a new stability. At the moment of the click a bright light shoots past your vision and vanishes into the darkness beyond. You realize that whatever it was that you just did, someone somewhere died as a result. You are horrified, but the angel steadies you, pointing out to you that you worked unconditionally: you did what was needed to be done to restore balance, and you did not move the piece with the full knowledge and therefore human decision. You mediated a fate action that changed a lot of things to restore a balance to a land somewhere in time.

The angel places a hand upon each of your shoulders and grasps you hard. You are immediately spun around at high speed until the breath is sucked from your lungs, and you find yourself fighting for breath. You begin to feel a strong stinging on your face and your hand reaches up to feel sand hitting your face at high speed. The wind slowly dies enough for you to grasp a breath, and you open your eyes to find yourself standing on the edge of the Abyss which is behind you, and the Inner Desert which is before you. The angel lets go of your shoulder and places a hand over your eyes so that you can see with the sight of angels. Before you is an immense construct of shapes and patterns with threads leading off in all directions. The angel begins to walk you down the Inner Desert, passing through

4. The magical dynamics of fate

the construct. As you pass through each shape, you feel the potential within it for a life event or a crossing of paths.

You are walked slowly down the Inner Desert until you come to a threshold you had never noticed before. As soon as your feet touch the threshold, you once again see in different ways through each eye. In one eye you see the patterns morphing and changing, every one renewing themselves in a dance of fate. In the other eye you see the world, a place, a person with their life intersecting with other people and events. You watch as the movement of the chess piece you instigated on the board begins to play out and change the life path of the person and all the events that it triggers. You see the old life path they were walking crumble and dissipate and a new path open up for them. Beyond the person, you see how the change in fate changed the whole world around them and restore a balance to a land, a community and a family line.

Once the angel is sure that you have seen all that you need to see, he turns you around and walks you back to the edge of the Abyss, where a large angel is waiting for you. The angel you stand before gives you a scroll of knowledge for you to absorb, which will unravel throughout your life to slowly expose you to the ancient Mysteries of fate and life patterns. You take the scroll, unsure what to do with it. The angel tells you to eat it, which you do. The scroll nestles itself in your body and will unfold in your mind over time as the information hidden within it is needed. The angel then grabs you hard by the arm and throws you over the edge of the Abyss. You begin to fall and a sense of utter terror rises within you as you realize you are potentially going to die. You fall down the Abyss, but the speed of your fall is slowed, enabling you to see all the tunnels and areas of the Abyss where the ancient beings of the distant past of our world are slumbering.

In their faces you see echoes of humanity, fragments that have survived time and emerged in the various species alive in your world today. You fall is slowed even more and you become aware of a funnel of wind forming in the Abyss and stretching high up past you and beyond the Inner Desert where you were standing. It reaches far up into the mists into the distant future where the angelic patterns of fate are woven. You are caught in the funnel of wind and you become aware of a soul in the funnel with you, a bright, beautiful power of life

4.3. The board game

that is half slumbering on its journey into a new life. You instinctively wrap yourself around the soul to protect it, and as you draw closer to the soul you become deeply aware of the beauty and stillness of the soul that you are protecting.

You watch as angelic beings that are the funnel watch over you both while also pulling on ancient bloodlines deep within the Abyss, triggering them out of hibernation and pulling in fragments of their development and evolution ready for the bloodlines that will be within the being as it manifests into life. A bright light shines up from below you: you slow even more and find that the funnel is coming to a completion at a threshold that was the same one in the Inner Desert where you stood. You are confused, as you have fallen a great depth into the Abyss and yet you are ending up presumably where you first started. The angels around you nudge you, which awakens the scroll within you, and you become aware that the soul will manifest in the Inner Desert of Humanity where you were working, but back in a time long before your humanity existed. Falling into the depths has taken you back into the distant past, into a world that will eventually lead to the present that you were witnessing being formed in the Inner Desert.

The brightness below you suddenly gets a lot brighter and you begin to hear a cacophony of sound, like a choir of voices that guide the funnel towards the bright light and awaken the soul that is nestled in your arms. The soul moves, like a sleepy child, and you are loath to let the child go, but the pull of the light gets too strong for you to cope with and you release the soul, watching it fall into the bright light and vanish. The funnel suddenly makes a loud whooshing sound as it vanishes, and you fall into a room where two people are making love. Angelic beings stand around ensuring the safe passage of the soul into the body of the woman, and you watch as her soul adjusts to accommodate the new soul in a complex yet gentle dance of energy.

The beings all around you and the couple watch impassively to ensure that the soul is properly placed within the woman, and you watch the light of the soul and the light of the woman's soul blend into a profusion of colour and sound. The angel touches you upon the shoulder and asks you to act in the role of sacred priest/ess and bless the soul of both the mother and child. You walk towards the woman and place a hand upon her head. Time, fate and the sounds

4. The magical dynamics of fate

of the frequency of the child's future flow through your hand into the woman, and you call upon the blessings of Divine Power to descend to them both, and for the strength of the Underworld to ascend to them. A mark appears upon her forehead and your work is done. Both their sacred paths are sealed, and nothing shall interfere with the future path of these two heavily interwoven souls.

The angel turns you around and around, turning you through the worlds and through time. You spin in a flow of life and death, of manifestation and completion, your own sound calling out through all the worlds. You spin into the Void, spinning in silence, coming slowly to stillness in the deep nothing. In that moment of stillness, you are aware of all the lives you have passed through as your soul manifests again and again throughout time, answering the call to life as you journey through yourself. The knowledge of that journey stays with you as you step instinctively from the Void and back into the life where you are sitting now before a candle flame. You watch the candle flame with your inner vision, seeing the power of Divine Being shine out of that light—you reach forward, gently lifting that sacred flame and placing it, once more, deep within you.

The flame fills you with peace and stillness, the Divine Power filling you with life as you open your eyes and consider the physical flame. You blow the flame out, sending it back into the Void, sitting for a moment to remember the long and difficult service and learning you have just been exposed to.

★ ★ ★

From that long and detailed vision, you will draw understanding of the act of fate, the falling into life of souls, and the sacred act of union that stretches up the Abyss in search of a soul to bring into life. This sacred act of union was used to bring the sacred kings and priestess-queens into life, to ensure the land always had a manifestation of Divinity within substance among the people.

The patterns that are woven at the edge of the Abyss are complex ones of power, intent, and interface. The shapes and threads are essentially angelic beings placed together in an ever-shifting pattern that filters the power of Divinity into the world, and from which life potential, with all its inherent possibilities, can flow. It's a bit like the

4.3. The board game

concept of stem cells: there is potential for many areas of growth and renewal. The pattern is often woven either by other angelic beings, or by deities. Often when you get a powerful god or goddess that is also associated with weaving, it is not talking about weaving baskets—that is a common modern interpretation that is just plain wrong—it is the weaving of existence. The deity pulls the threads of angelic consciousness together and the weave will decide how the power will manifest: will it be a human or a tree? Divine Power utters out of the Void, passes through the weave of angelic consciousness that is woven by a deity, and becomes manifest. How that manifestation will interact both with Divine Power and everything else around it is where the fate pattern comes in. Fate does not decide who we are: it provides materials for us to build with.

Fate can deal you many bad or good cards: it is how you use each card that truly decides your fate. In magic, for adepts, the deeper into the Inner Worlds you go, the heavier and stronger the impact of fate becomes, for a variety of reasons. The more you can process and carry, the heavier your burden will be. The more you call through the worlds for wisdom, the more obstacles and challenges you will be woven. Wisdom comes from struggle and bitter experience, not from love and hugs. If you become a consecrated priest, then more fate lines are woven into your 'cloth' to enable you to be in the places you need to be in to achieve your role as priest. The higher the power levels you become able to access, the more dangerous your fate becomes: this ensures the swift severing of the life threads should a priest abuse the power of Divine Being. A good mythical picture of this is the sword of Damocles. The Roman politician and philosopher Cicero tells the famous story about the Syracusan tyrant Dionysius II and his courtier Damocles, a story which Cicero had read in the *History* of Timaeus of Tauromenium. The story was originally a peek at the Mystery of the Fate of Kings, but it eventually degenerated down to a moral story.

> Pandering to his king, Damocles exclaimed that, as a great man of power and authority surrounded by magnificence, Dionysius was truly fortunate. Realizing the stupidity of this courtier, Dionysius offered to switch places with him, so he could taste first hand that fortune.

4. THE MAGICAL DYNAMICS OF FATE

> Damocles could think of no other place he would rather be and accepted the King's proposal. Damocles sat down in the king's throne surrounded by every luxury, but Dionysius arranged that a huge sword should hang above the throne, held at the pommel only by a single hair of a horse's tail. Damocles finally begged the king that he be allowed to leave, as he no longer wanted to be so fortunate.

In the story that is told today, the king himself had the sword hung above the head of Damocles. In the Mysteries of Fate, the sword does indeed hang over the heads of those at the height of power, both in kingship and priesthood, but the sword is there by the grace of the deity of Justice: the swift sword of justice hangs by a thin thread, just as the scales are balanced by a feather. The more power you are given access to, the greater the destruction if you consciously fail or become corrupt. The powers of Fate and Justice are two of the same threads of power expression: they ensure balance and harmony.

When you become a magical teacher, or magical adept, or hierophant/magus/whatever, you take on a greater burden of responsibility. The willingness to be of service at a high level brings with it great power but also great responsibility. The more power you wield, and the more you have access to, the thinner the thread that holds the sword. Should you knowingly do something that upsets the inner order/pattern, or hurts a being out of sheer malice, greed or corruption, or manipulates fate for your own selfish means, then the sword will come crashing down upon you. It is a fail-safe device that protects the integrity of Divine Power within Humanity, and its falling is not a punishment, it is a severing of the umbilicus that connects you to the power source to stop you having access to unnecessary destruction. You become powerless, which is itself a terrible blow.

When working with this power it is very important to understand that morality and our human sense of right and wrong have nothing to do with the powers of fate and justice. Things that we may consider evil flow into the world to create change, to bring about massive destruction: genocide, war and oppression. Power is constantly flowing in many directions and we have to step back to observe the effect that the power has upon us. Sometimes such destruction is needed; sometimes it is not. Sometimes struggling against some injustice brings about a major change in the consciousness of the people, which could not have happened any other way.

As a magician, when such destruction and oppression is happening purely out of human imbalance, then you cannot act magically to change it. You can, however, act magically to bring it to a conclusion, it is just that you cannot mould that conclusion. You give power to the situation to do whatever it needs to do to bring about an unconditional conclusion: you cannot dictate the outcome. If you work that way, then you can lessen the suffering in that you shorten the time span of the process without interfering in the end product. Even if you do not like the end product, you must not interfere, as fate often has long arms that stretch way into the future, way beyond your ability to see the whole pattern.

If, however, magic is being used to manipulate a large pattern or event—World War II is a good example of this—then all bets are off regarding the path of fate: you can do whatever needs to be done. During World War II both the Germans and the British were using magic to influence the outcome of the war. Hitler's use of drugs (amphetamines), combined with his very fateful soul which was walking a mental tightrope, ensured that when the magical doors were opened, a whole stream of powerful parasites and then demonic beings flowed into feed off of the situation. It was magic that tipped the situation over the cliff, so magic could be used to put the brakes on.

If a fate is very strong, then there is really very little that can be done to alter it, and it probably should not be interfered with anyhow. You will find, when looking at a strong and important fate pattern in a person, that if you block one route, then another will open with similar details within the pattern. The details are always silly inconsequential ones, but act as beacons for the powers of fate to flow through.

4.4 Summary

Really, at the end of the day, we know so little that it is best to not try and interfere, but just restore balance where some other idiot has

4. THE MAGICAL DYNAMICS OF FATE

tried to interfere. The magic of fate is a complex and powerful area of magic, and the best learning can be gained from going into the inner patterns and simply observing. So much more makes sense once you have experienced the powers that flow through the pattern, and to observe the making of a pattern of fate is one of the most beautiful and awe-inspiring experiences I think a human can have.

And when you are faced with the pattern of your own fate and it is one that you do not like, then tough shit basically. You will know you are growing in your magical maturity when you stop trying to alter your fate in a major way and start working with it to achieve whatever it is you need to achieve. Every path has something to teach us, something that will make us stronger and wiser. To try and foreshorten that, or dodge all bad things, is complete folly and will actually take away the gifts that are given when you walk a rocky path. You can, however, look to see where your mistakes or bad decisions may appear, and head them off by learning the lesson consciously. Or at times, when prompted, you can step to one side of a disaster when it is not necessary for you to go through it. The trick is to understand the complexity of cause and effect, and to know what to sidestep and what to take on the chin.

The harder you put your shoulder to the boulder of fate to push, the greater the rewards that eventually trickle down to you when the time is right. Of all the many disasters that have happened in my life, looking back, I would not change a second of them. Everything, and I mean everything, down to the smallest detail, taught me something, gave me strength, learning, smacks around the head when I needed them, and opened future paths to wonderful things. To see all of that dynamic in action from an inner point of view, to me, is the highlight of a magician's career.

Chapter Five

How to work with angels: bound, religious, part human and natural

The other two Magical Knowledge books both have chapters regarding the nature of angelic beings and some of their functions, so we will not need to cover that ground again here. Instead, I would like to take the time to look at the various forms of angels that magicians come into contact with through the course of a lifetime, how they came to those forms and how to address those forms. Then we will look at working methods for working with angelic beings and within angelic structures.

This will give us a deeper understanding of how some magical and religious structures hang together and why. To work at an adept level with angelic beings, you really need to know what it is you are working with, why you are working with them and what will be the likely outcome. To blindly walk into the circle of work with angels without those basic foundational understandings will limit the power and breadth of the magical work, and if it is a religious structure, will severely limit the religion's ability to connect with Divine Being.

I have chosen the three most likely forms of angelic beings that a magician will encounter and we will look at them in turn. The bound angels are angelic beings that have, over time, been bound into service by priest-magicians to serve the agenda of the religion and the priesthood. The most common occurrence of this began back around 1500 B.C. and by 500 B.C. it was a commonplace practice within certain ancient priesthoods. I am talking about the areas that we would call the Near East, the various Mediterranean cultures and as far east as northwest India. I cannot comment on the rest of the world as I have had no direct working experience with bound angels

5. How to work with angels: bound, religious, part human and natural

from other cultures, but I have no reason to think that it was not happening elsewhere.

5.1 Bound angels

A bound angel has had its function 'tightened' and focused, and it is not free to act naturally. The bindings force the angel to fulfil its function to the whims and agenda of the priesthood that has bound it. This was very successfully done in ancient times and the method of working with such beings was handed down the generations. By the 11th century onward, the fact that these beings were actually in bondage had been forgotten and the names, working methods and functions of the angelic beings had become a 'truth': the early Kabbalists for example had no idea they were working with beings that had been bound and moulded to work with them. Because of this, it encouraged the development of a form of magical interaction that was inherently abusive and relied heavily on a form of inner slavery. This is very evident in the Keys of Solomon and the whole Solomonic stream of magic.

So how were these angels bound in the first place? The key to this answer is in the Torah and the Pentateuch: man is an octave or echo of Divinity and has the power of utterance to create and destroy. Angels are functional beings who have individual purposes and are answerable to God and Man. To adapt such a being is fairly easy if you know how: these beings only exist to serve, have no emotional structure and have access to vast reserves of power. If a human utters a command using the utterance of God, and uses words that bind and direct, then it will change the structure of the angelic being without a struggle: we are echoes of Divinity and Divinity commands the angels. The interesting aside of all this is that Man is within Divinity and Divinity is within Man, and there are also cases where Man has become angelic, which we will go into later.

The angelic being is bound using sacred language and then is directed by command. The angel can only do whatever it is that is its natural function. So for example, an angel of death can only take life, it cannot give life or provide substance, change the weather, etc. The binding will give the magician the power to use that angel of death

5.1. Bound angels

as a weapon against nations and individuals. In nature, the angelic beings that work in death act as doorways for people and creatures as is dictated by the flow and pattern of fate. They cannot be stopped or directed in any way: they are like a wind that sweeps the land clean. But once bound, they often cannot answer that call of fate and instead are only able to function at the direction of their master or the priestly line which holds the control. I have however come across some bound angels who seem to at least partially function in their natural capacity but are still bound when called upon.

The bound angels present themselves as images of function, have names, hierarchies and a very distinctive appearance. These are the angels that have been bound for so long that people have forgot the fact that they are bound and assume that the appearance and name is the actual angel, which is incorrect. Purely naturally occurring angelic beings have no name, only a signature sound, and do not tend to have any form of humanlike appearance. If an angel appears before you in a human-type form it is one of three things: either it is bound, or it is dressing up so that you can interact with it, or it is an angelic being that has a fragment of humanity within it. The way to tell if it is bound or not is to simply ask it: if it cannot change its appearance, then chances are it is bound.

If you get the urge to unbind it, first find out what it does in its natural form. Some angelic beings were bound up to prevent them from massacring whole populations or wiping out species. It's a difficult dilemma really, because such angelic beings are basically fulfilling the natural balance of the planet and keeping everything healthy. If something overgrows, then it is weeded back. But if you are one of those weeds, then there is a self-interest in survival which may prevent you from wanting to unbind it.

Then there is the issue of naturally bound angels which are angelic beings that are bound and held in the Inner Desert to prevent them working until the time is right. Then when it is time for them to do their job, they are released from the bondage of the Inner Desert so that they can once again walk the earth.

If you are truly not sure, then you can work in vision, going into the Inner Desert, to the area of binding and severity where there are many bound angels and other beings, and ask the guardian

5. How to work with angels: bound, religious, part human and natural

and attendant workers there for their opinion and advice. They are angelic beings themselves and their task is to ensure that beings, including angelic beings that have no place currently in our world are held in binding until it is time for release. If you come across a bound angel and get the urge to unbind them, then it is a good idea to check that it has not been naturally bound or bound by man under the instruction of Divinity.

There is no set method for unbinding an angel: you have to work from instinct, as the methods of binding are many and complex. The basic rule of thumb is, work in vision: first get the angel to agree regarding the unbinding, look for sigils or text somewhere on the body, or it can be on a thread that is tied to the leg, neck, arm, etc. of the angel. It could also be written on a strip of cloth and hung down its throat. But somewhere on the body will be the utterance that bound it. Removing the utterance will depend upon what element of magic was used in the initial binding. You may have to blow off the script, eat it, wipe it clean with tears, or scratch it off: it will be a very physical action and it will have physical repercussions upon your body. You will know when you have been successful because the angel will completely transform itself. Then you will be able to converse with the angel and ask it who bound it and why. Unbinding like this is a major spiritual service, but before you go rushing off to save the angel world, be aware that the bodily impact, that usually slams in a day or two after, is really not a pleasant experience. After you have done such work you will really need to clean up, so take a ritual salt bath.

You may find it interesting once you have unbound an angel to ask it questions about the nature of its work as a bound angel, what it did, why and for whom. You could also ask the angel, while you have its attention, what did it do before it was bound, what was its primary purpose, and ask the angel to show you through its eyes how it worked. It can be a massive learning experience. It would also be prudent to ask the angel how to call it. They don't actually have names—those were all given to them by humans—but they do have signature sounds that are unique to them. If you ask the angel, it will make the sound that identifies it, and it will put that sound in your head. If it is within range of your voice, you can then physically use the sound to call the angel if you really need to. If the sound is completely out of range of human hearing or voice capabilities, then you will have to 'think' the sound in your head: the effect will be the same. But only call these angels if you really need it to do something that is specifically within their function range, and even then you can only ask, do not command: by commanding, you take on the mantle of God and you are not God, not matter how much your girlfriend tells you that you are.

5.2 Religious angels

Religious angels are angelic beings that operate completely within a religious structure and uphold it. They are not bound and they work mainly by cooperation to facilitate an interface by which man can talk to Divinity, be it a god or goddess. The structure of a religious angel is basically a presentation of a humanlike being with a specific name, wide brief of function and occasionally attendant emotive qualities. The angel, unlike a bound angel, agrees freely as part of its service to dress in a way and function in a way that upholds the inner and outer structure of a religion which acts as an interface between Humanity and Divinity.

The angel presents itself in its assigned role in a way that enables the human to understand the function and intention of the angelic being, and the assigned interface allows the human to request, commune with and generally build a relationship with that angelic being within the sphere of its function, and beyond that a communion with Divinity. This dance will continue while ever the religion truly acts as a bridge between man and God. It is not dependant upon dogma, creed etc., but purely the fact that an inner structure was built to accommodate an outer structure upon which was placed a religion that worked. So it does not matter which deity the religion is working with, or what its 'rules' are, so long as it actually works from the human side, and as long as the humans involved, i.e. the priesthood, are doing what they are supposed to be doing, then the angelic beings play the game. They usually facilitate communication, companionship: bring healing, bridge death and birth, all the usual angelic functions, just within a specific religious structure.

5. How to Work with Angels: Bound, Religious, Part Human and Natural

If the human part of the bargain ceases to operate, i.e. it becomes totally corrupt and no longer serves Divinity, then the angelic beings slowly withdraw first from the outer expressions, and then from the upholding of the inner structure. The religion becomes an empty shell with no power and eventually crumbles. When that happens, the angelic beings slowly cast off the 'dressing' of that religion and return to their more natural appearance. Their function stays the same, it just does not operate through a religious window.

When a religion is first put together, or when a major temple is first built, the priesthood would work in vision and ritual with angelic beings, using them as foundations for the Inner Temple and outer temple. The following vision is something I worked with many years ago, and is a very good example of how this method of construction works. It demonstrates the inner construction of a Catholic cathedral which would be done before the outer building itself is worked on. It will show you how Angelic powers and Divine presence are brought through into an inner structure to create a sacred place.

The vision of the cathedral is using the inner flow of the power of the East to manifest itself through a Christian Mystery. The details of the religious outcomes are irrelevant: it could be a mosque or a Greek Temple. It doesn't matter. The knowledge and ability to open the power of the elemental temple and work with the powers that flow through that mediation is what is important.

The form it will take (Christian, Muslim, pagan) is a surface detail that takes form as the power exteriorizes. It is the moulding that is done as the power comes through. Each variation still has the same rules: this is how you open the door, this is how you use a deity to mediate the power, this is how beings can work like building blocks.

So, as you will see, the vision gives you the feel of how it is done. If any of you go to the south of England, go to Wells Cathedral. When you stand in the west and look east, you will see how the architect has actually placed the power patterns of the Angelic Beings in the building. You can see their pattern right there in front of you.

I stood there once, waiting from my daughters to finish looking at something, and I sort of glazed over. But when I came back into focus I saw them for the first time and was astounded. I had been there so many times and not noticed. How could I have been so blind? (And stupid!) But then, I seem to specialize in random acts of complete stupidity, so I guess it was to be expected.

5.3 The consecration of the cathedral

Light a candle and meditate on the inner flame that burns deep within you. As you look at the central flame it grows bigger and bigger until you are seated before a column of fire. You are drawn to the fire and find yourself stepping through the fire with the intent of going to the creation of the cathedral.

Stepping over the threshold you find yourself standing before a beautiful cathedral that is still under construction. It is all but finished, and detailed carving is being added to the outside the building. The priests and priestesses stream into the building and you follow.

Inside, it is filled with people who are weaving threads and connecting them from one end of the building to another. They are pulling threads from a central point and weaving an inner matrix for power to pass through. Once it is completed you are urged to go and kneel before the altar. You can feel that the altar is not yet consecrated or tuned to any specific power. Many of the people kneel with you and tell you to turn inward, to meditate on the central flame.

You pass into stillness and stay in a place of silence and peace. A power builds up all around you and within you. Urgency passes through your mind and you can feel the need to do something, but you are not sure what. You begin to cough as air forces its way out of your lungs. The force becomes too much and you tip your head back to allow a sound to release from your body. You cry a cry that comes from every cell in your body. It is the cry of hopelessness, despair and imbalance: the human separated from the rest of existence.

A call and a movement answer the cry. The east wall of the cathedral falls away and is replaced by light. As you adjust to the light, you realize the light is coming from a woman who stands on the threshold of the east. At her head are the stars and at her feet is the moon. She stretches out her arms, and her robe falls open. The opened robe reveals the Void within her, a place from which all light, all being, and all compassion steams.

5. How to Work with Angels: Bound, Religious, Part Human and Natural

Out of the light step two large Angelic beings that stand opposite each other. They stretch out their wings to touch, reaching beyond the ceiling of the cathedral. They reach out and touch hands, crossing their arms at the wrist and they both move one foot forward until their toes are touching. They create a double helix pattern with their bodies, which upholds the building and enlivens the web pattern.

Once the angels are in place, another being steps out of the East. You see the outline of a human shape, but the inner fire of this being is so bright that you cannot see any detail. The human comes up to you and touches you on the forehead. A light of immense intensity flows through you and you feel that you might die in a state of joy. As your body adjusts to the light, you feel awakened and at peace.

The human then goes to the Altar and lies upon the cold stone. Their body sinks into the Altar, becoming one with the stone: becoming the Corpus Christi. You rise to your feet and go to stand before the Altar with your hands resting lightly on the stone. You feel the stone beneath you breathe and the power of peace and stillness flows from the stone into you.

A priest touches you lightly on the shoulder and tells you that it is time to leave. As you turn to go, you realize that many priests are praying in the cathedral: priests of the time and place of the cathedral. You move quietly towards the west door and pass through a threshold of fire.

The fire passes through you as you cross the threshold and you feel the power of the guardian as you step from one world to another. You emerge back in the room where you first started. When you are ready, you open your eyes and meditate on the candle flame for a moment before blowing it out.

★ ★ ★

The angelic beings and the priesthood work in tandem to create images and actions of the angelic beings, and after that, decades and millennia of generations interacting with that construct serves to strengthen it. In actuality, those presentations are merely windows through which we can converse with the angelic being and through that being, interact with Divinity, or receive an intervention of Divinity through the mediation of the angelic being.

In some ancient temples, early cathedrals and Norman churches, the angelic interface is still there if you know how to turn the lights on. Later buildings and even some ancient temples are completely empty or closed down and really it is just a matter of testing the light switch in each place you go to and seeing if it is still active or not. There is really no other way of judging which ones are still running and which ones are not. Going into a church, cathedral or temple, sitting in vision and seeing the inner structure will tell you a great deal, then opening the gates in the east will confirm whether the angelic structure is still active or not. You will also be able to see the religious dressing of the angelic beings as they were when they first began their 'tour of service' with that religion, and it can be interesting to contrast that image with later artistic interpretations in the religious community as the culture slowly changed.

5.4 Religious angels of recitation

The three main monotheistic religions that come out of the Near East all use the power of the word as their foundation. All three religions, Christianity, Islam and Judaism, have recitation and a book as their central focus. The angelic beings that are the thresholds for that power of the Word are beings that are important to work with from an esoteric point of view. They will teach you the deeper mysteries of recitation and the power of the Word. The following vision will teach you about recitation and what recitation is really about. It is within a framework of the monotheistic religions and the name God is used in the context of Divine consciousness without gender or form.

5.5 The vision of recitation

Light a candle flame in the east and close your eyes. See the flame with your inner vision and allow yourself to be drawn into the flame. Find yourself stood within the flame, bathing in the cold fire of the Void, from which all comes and to which all returns. Look out beyond the flame and see a threshold to a temple of the east. Its columns and threshold are guarded by large angelic beings with many eyes and many wings. Step out of the fire and stand before the two guardians,

5. How to Work with Angels: Bound, Religious, Part Human and Natural

bow to them and step onto the threshold. You feel the threshold beneath you, which is also an angelic being, and you feel the threshold looking into your soul, looking over your life and looking into your mind to see your intentions.

Stand on the threshold of the East and when the guardians of the thresholds step back, walk over the threshold and into the temple. You begin to walk down a long columned walkway, many guardians watching you as you walk. A wind begins to blow. The wind gets stronger and stronger until you have to lean into the wind to fight through the wind to reach two great doors in the distance.

The wind takes the breath from your lungs and you battle against the hurricane that stings your eyes and suffocates you. You reach the great doors of the inner sanctum, which is also the source of the wind. Something with you tells you to place your forehead to the great doors and you can feel the doors looking into you, seeing if you are honourable enough to be allowed to pass through them. Just as you begin to think you have failed, the great doors swing open and before you is the Void with a whirlwind blowing from it. The wind sucks you in and you fall through the wind, twisting and turning. The wind seems to have arms that hold you as you fall until you hit a sandy floor with a thump.

Standing up, you find yourself in a small empty cubic building. The aged walls are covered with many small rough-cut niches. The niches are empty and you know that you must fill them, but you are not sure what with. Go up to the walls and run your hands over the niches. They feel beautiful and strange.

You become aware that an angel is behind you. You feel the presence and power all around you. The angel leans against you. Power builds up within you, forcing breath from your lungs until your body screams for oxygen. Colour drains from your face and nausea assaults your throat. You cannot inhale.

The angel grabs you by the hair and shouts in your ear:

> Recite! Recite what God commands you. Recite the words that the Angels brought to the world and uttered before the throne of God. Recite so that thy soul shall never forget. Recite from the depths of thy heart where

> the words of God are written upon the souls of all beings.
> Recite so that all worlds and all times shall hear what we
> have given to those who would listen. Recite the song of
> Paradise so that all shall behold its beauty.

Open your mouth and inhale. The oxygen hits your brain, exploding light throughout your mind that weaves its way to your lips, forcing out words that you cannot understand. The words take form and travel across the surface of the room, mingling with the angel who joins the recitation.

The word forms become shapes and settle in the niches creating a light of their own. Each word form becomes a deity, an expression of Divinity, flowing with the power of the Void. When the niches are full, the room dances with brilliant light and you finally understand that it is Paradise upon Earth as you bathe in the power and beauty that surrounds you.

Each word shines with the light of power. The power of the Void flows through each word as each word takes a form. The angel passes a hand over your face and tells you to look through his fingers.

You see a door that you had not noticed before. As you touch the door, it moves and breathes, causing you to step back. The door transforms into a light which is so bright that it burns all images from your mind. The angel holds out his hand and speaks to the light:

> Hail Ridwan, keeper of the doors of Paradise, threshold
> to the Throne of God. May this mortal pass through you
> and still be as one being. May they leave Paradise and
> hold its secrets on their lips throughout eternity.

The light dims and the angel pushes you forward. You fall into the door and find yourself enveloped by the power of the Angel of Paradise. In the depths of this power, the Angel speaks to you about your immortal self, and you commune together in silence.

The power of the Angel burns through you and for a moment you see yourself in your entirety, through all lives in all worlds. Within the vision of yourself you see Paradise: the first expression of Divinity as it emerges out of the Void.

5. How to work with angels: bound, religious, part human and natural

Ridwan, Keeper of the doors of Paradise, opens himself and you tumble through the doors to find yourself falling through fire. Looking down you see the Earth below you and you fall towards it at great speed. As the planet gets nearer, you hear many whispers and feel the hands of people reaching out to touch you.

The Earth gets closer and closer until you fall towards a city, a street and finally a building. You pass through the roof of the building and end back in the room where you first started. You fill the whole room and look down with difficulty at the tiny body that you have been living in. Breathing deeply, you begin to draw yourself in, a step at a time.

Slowly, you shrink yourself down until you are the same size as your body. You begin to realize just how limited your true expression is while you are in a body. When you are ready, you open your eyes and look around you. Be aware of all the Divine expressions of power in the living beings, plants and rocks around you. Gently blow the candle out, sending the flame back into the Void.

5.6 Human angels

The next kind of angel to look at has fragments of humanity within it. Don't ask me how this happens because I do not have a bloody clue, but there are many inner beings such as angels, demons and deities to name a few that were once upon a time human.

There are humans who, probably by nature of their magical work, but that is only a guess, end up somehow morphing over time in the Inner Worlds into angelic beings. It may be that they are a construct within themselves, i.e. created as beings that have humanity as well as angelic qualities so that they can be duel interfaces in the depths of the Inner Desert, the place where humanity is formed. But again, that is just an idea really.

My direct experience of them has been in the Inner Desert, by the Abyss and in the Abyss. They combine the focused power of an angel with some emotive quality of humanity and the ability to communicate openly with humanity. The Sandalphon and Metatron are both the most well known ones in Biblical terms but also the most reported in inner visions by magicians and mystics. They are perceived as very large humanlike angelic beings that will converse, protect and teach humans in inner vision. They work closely with those who are working in service in the Inner Worlds, and Metatron appears to be tied to the Abyss and unable to pass beyond that. He is the bridge between our side of the Abyss and the side of Divinity. The Sandalphon however work in the Inner Desert but also upon the surface of the planet. The interesting question would be, would they still exist if humanity did not? Are they tied or a part of our humanity or are they independent of us?

When working in vision with these forms of angels, it is very interesting that they show a full understanding of the emotive nature of humanity, which all other angels do not. Because of that, they also have a great insight into out failings, our bullshit, and our agendas: they cannot be fooled and they can get angry, which makes them very dangerous. Let's look a bit closer at a human angelic form.

5.7 Sandalphon/Synadalphos ("colleague")

Sandalphon is an angelic being of the Earth. Their action is parallel to the Watchers who befriend humanity and teach the human race what they need to know. Sandalphon is a being who walks with humanity and guides them. Sandalphon is also referred to as the gardener: he who tends and nurtures. The following vision introduces you to Sandalphon and gives you a way to work with this power.

5.8 Vision of the Companion

Light the candle and meditate on the power of the flame for a while. Be aware of the strengthening of your own inner flame. The central flame grows bigger and you are drawn to step through the fire. As you step through the fire you find yourself walking through an Inner Desert and an angel begins to walk alongside you

You walk for a while in silence before you ask the angel who he is. The angel stops and looks at you. He places his hands across your eyes and tells you to look through his hands. His voice resonates through you head like a drumbeat.

5. How to work with angels: bound, religious, part human and natural

> I am the angel of the earth upon which you walk. I am the skin across the soil, the grains of sand in the Inner Desert: I am he who lies between the stars and the Underworld. I am around and within you. I am completion.

With that the angel takes you by the arm and walks you at great speed across the Inner Desert. You flow upon and also through the sand, which seems to almost pass through you as you walk. The sand interacts with your flesh, and you lose sense of where your flesh ends the sand begins. The angel stands you in the centre of the Inner Desert and points to the Abyss in the distance. He then turns you and points to the mountains in the distance in the opposite direction. He then takes your hand and places it upon his head. You feel many things through your hand: you feel the bark of trees, the strength of rocks, the rich earth, and grains of sand. You feel flesh, your own flesh within the angel.

The angel then takes you to the edge of a great city wall and points to it. You are confused for a moment until you look closer and see the angel is also part of the great city wall. He is truly all around you. You talk to the angel and ask him what you need to know. When you have finished, the angel walks you towards a mist that has gathered in a section of the Inner Desert. He walks you into the mist and when you get so deep into the mist that you cannot see anything, the angel leaves you. You flounder for a short while until you remember the Void within everything.

You step forward with the intention of stepping into the Void. You find yourself with nothing, within stillness and silence. You stand in peace, in stillness, and realize this is your natural state: total stillness and silence. Something reminds you that you must step forward back into life and with that you take a step forward out of the Void with the intention to go back to your body. As you step into the room where you first started, you look around and see fragments of the angel in all the things around you, in the floor, the walls: he is all around you and within you. When you are ready you open your eyes and touch the floor in recognition of Sandalphon: the skin of the Earth.

5.9 Metatron

Metatron is written about as being the prophet Enoch who walked with God and was not. He is one of the angels who was once a man, and he holds the great seat of power before the throne of God. In the Tree of Life he is the one who stands in the Abyss and is the bridge between God and humanity. He is often referred to as the Prince of Countenance. The name Metatron seems to have no roots in any language and to date no one really knows where the name came from.

> Sitting next to God, Enoch was instructed in wisdom, and using his skills as a scribe, prepared three hundred and sixty-six books. When he learned everything, a most significant thing happened. God revealed to him great secrets: some of which are even kept secret from the angels. These included the secrets of Creation, the duration of time the world will survive, and what will happen after its demise. At the end of these discussions, Enoch returned to earth for a limited time, to instruct everyone, including his sons, in all he learned. After thirty days, the angels returned him to Heaven.
>
> And then the divine transformation took place. Additional wisdom and spiritual qualities caused Enoch's height and breadth to become equal to the height and breadth of the earth. God attached thirty-six wings to his body, and gave him three hundred and sixty-five eyes, each as bright as the sun. His body turned into celestial fire: flesh, veins, bones, hair, all metamorphosed to glorious flame. Sparks emanated from him, and storms, whirlwind, and thunder encircled his form. The angels dressed him in magnificent garments, including a crown, and arranged his throne. A heavenly herald proclaimed that from then on his name would no longer be Enoch, but Metatron, and that all angels must obey him, as second only to God.
>
> — *The Legends of the Jews*, by Louis Ginsberg.

5. How to work with angels: bound, religious, part human and natural

So Metatron is a powerful Mystery who bridges for us the realms of divinity and humanity. The following vision takes us to the edge of the Void where we can reach out to communication with the power Metatron. The depth of his humanity allows us close contact with such an immense being without being destroyed.

5.10 The vision of Metatron and the Abyss

Be still and light a candle. As you become silent, so you begin to lose awareness of the room in which you are seated. The external noises fade, your mind settles and your breathing becomes relaxed and natural. Using your inner vision, you look at the candle flame before you. The room in which you are seated falls away and you find yourself looking through the flame to a landscape beyond.

Instinctively you reach through the flame and pass into the landscape—a place of sand, earth and wind. The wind whips around you and the sand gets into your eyes. For a moment you are blinded and yet you become aware of someone walking alongside you. As your eyes clear, you see a humanlike being, neither male nor female, walking alongside you, and yet their feet are down in the earth, so their legs are only visible from the calf up. They walk through the earth as though it was not there. Their hair is long and trails along the ground behind them, swishing away their footprints. No mark is left of their passing.

The being reaches out to touch you, and as their hand contacts your skin, a force flows through you with such strength that you fear you may fall. You become aware of the landscape in a different way. Life reflects from everything around you. The stones, the grains of sand, the plants and the wind, all are lit with the light of Divinity—all life is visible to you. Looking around you see people come and go: they are unaware of you as you observe them. The perfection of power manifest in substance is evident in every person you look upon, and as you look to your own hands, you see divinity within your own flesh.

The angel moves you on and you walk deeper and deeper into the Inner Desert, leaving the people behind. As you walk you become more and more aware of the mistakes you have made in this life, and

5.10. The vision of Metatron and the Abyss

the things that you have to learn. You find yourself assessing your life and you become so absorbed in this task that you arrive at the edge of a cliff without realizing. The angel puts out one arm to stop you falling over the edge. You look out over the cliff and see that it falls down so far that you cannot see the bottom. It looks like a tear in the universe with no end. You look up and the sky is the same. The tear rises up through the stars.

On the other side is a land swathed in mist. Something draws you to the other side but there is no way to cross. As you look around for a way across, a sound like no other echoes around the Abyss. The sound gets louder and louder until you put your hands over your ears. The angel who has walked beside you kneels down and lowers his head.

Out of the Abyss rises a being that looks like a man but is so large he fills the Abyss. He places one eyeball up to the cliff edge so that he can see you. He strains to see something so small but when he sees you he smiles and places out his hand. He whispers for you to step onto his hand but his voice is so strong it sounds like a hurricane strong enough to demolish the earth itself. Carefully you step out onto his hand and he holds you up so that he can see you better. He cannot speak to you lest his voice destroy you, so he reaches over and places you on the other side of the Abyss. As soon as your feet touch the floor the power of Divine presence flows through you and your mind fills with awareness. Things you had not been able to understand suddenly become clear and a deep, powerful peace rises within you.

Metatron lifts you back over the Abyss quickly before you can lose your sense of humanity: to stand upon the realm of God one must lose who they are. You are placed gently back on the ground beside the kneeling angel. The archangel Metatron holds a hand of blessing over you before withdrawing back into the Abyss. The blessing fills you with fire and heat, so much so that you feel you are standing within fire and yet you are filled with stillness.

The stillness stays with you as you remember being seated before a candle flame. Your focus returns to the candle and you see the Divinity and stillness flow through the flame. Carefully, you blow out the candle, allowing your breath to mingle with the fire and the flame

5. How to work with angels: bound, religious, part human and natural

passes from this world to a deeper one. Remain seated and quiet for a while, allowing the stillness to deepen within you before you rise.

5.11 Natural angels

Natural angels are my term for angelic beings that have not been messed around with by humanity and religions or magic. An angelic being in its natural form is a threshold being that enables something to manifest or unmanifest: they are thresholds, literally sometimes. They appear in strange forms, often in the shape of Platonic solids, or spinning wheels with many eyes, long threads with many eyes and ears, etc. Whenever they appear with human or animal form, then chances are they have been altered or have been working with a human religious or magical structure for a very long time.

The best way to observe natural angelic beings at work, as a magician, would be to observe them working at the edge of the Abyss, where humanity prepares to take on a manifest form. You will be able to see them interlinking, interconnecting, and weaving together to form an energy filter through which consciousness can flow on its way to become a manifest being in the world.

The Metatron Cube is an example of an angelic filter at work and its job is to specifically be a threshold for humanity. The Metatron Cube is a hive of angelic beings that create an intricate pattern through their interlinking and that series of patterns and shapes triggers a release of Divine Power across the Abyss that then passes through the Metatron Cube. As it passes through the pattern, the power is shaped, its consciousness is awakened, and the momentum of the burst of power across the Abyss sets off the pattern in motion. The pattern travels down the Inner Desert landscape (flowing down the Tree of Life) interacting with and triggering certain areas of the Inner Desert that hold specific powers (the spheres). Once it has reached the threshold of physical manifestation it is ready to be born. Stepping over the threshold of Malkuth, the human consciousness steps into birth and the Metatron cube holds the integrity of the soul's ability to manifest through the life of the human. When the human dies, the pattern begins to break up as the angelic beings pull apart the pattern.

The pattern, which is angelic consciousness, has many patterns within it, and those patterns have patterns within them too. Our ability to manifest is based upon the shapes, patterns, harmonic sounds and vibrations that we label angelic beings. Those shapes and harmonies have consciousness and we can interact with them. They do not however have emotions like we do: they have purpose and function and do not exist outside those functions. This focus of function allows them to handle vast amounts of power, which in turns allows the world to physically exist. We have a much wider scope of action, but we are more diffuse, hence we are much weaker when it comes to mediating power. We do however have a greater emotive and conscious ability then angelic beings.

So back to the pattern at the edge of the Abyss. The Metatron cube is a fascinating angelic construct to observe in action, and a lot can be learned about real natural angelic beings just by observing them at work. The following vision takes you to the threshold of the Abyss and allows you to observe the process of angelic mediation of life. One word of warning: do not be tempted to deviate from the vision and begin experimenting with this structure. Once you have observed and then worked with it for a while, then you will know exactly what you are doing and will be able to branch out with the work. In the initial phases of working in vision though, stick to the boundaries of the vision until you have a template to work with. Wandering around messing about with the pattern when you do not know what you are doing will result in you being fried both physically and mentally. It's a very strong visionary presence and is akin to standing right next to the biggest nuclear reactor that you can imagine.

5.12 The vision of the Metatron Cube

Light a candle and close your eyes. With your inner vision see the candle flame before you. You are drawn to the flame and find yourself stepping into the flame, which is cool and refreshing. You bathe in the flames, which fill you with energy and stillness. That stillness draws you to walk forward through the flame and into the Void. You pass into the deep nothing that all things flow from and flow to, the place where there is no time, no space and no movement. In this still

5. How to work with angels: bound, religious, part human and natural

place, your daily life falls away and you find the eternal you drifting in the stillness, spreading out beyond the boundaries of your humanity. Something calls to you within this still place and you find yourself stepping out of the Void with the intention of going into the Inner Desert.

You step out of the Void, stepping onto sand and finding the Sandalphon stood before you. The Sandalphon stands tall, their hair long and trailing in the sand behind them, and their bodies the colour of the sand around them. They motion for you to follow them, which you do and together, you set out walking towards the Abyss that is at the far end of the Inner Desert. At the other end is the River of Death.

The angel walks you to the edge of the Abyss and then turns you around to observe a pattern of human life going into manifestation. Before you, at the edge of the Abyss, strange shapes start to appear out of nowhere, their shapes being Platonic solids spinning at high speed. They give off a strange deep harmony that vibrates right through your body. They align themselves into a pattern of thirteen shapes, the spinning and vibration moving the shapes to where they need to be.

The angel moves you to one side, to get you out of the way of what is about to happen, but near enough that you can still see everything that is happening. From across the Abyss, the realm of Divinity, comes a wind like a breath. A deep mist, a mist that does not seem to be affected by the wind, obscures the other side of the Abyss: you cannot see anything, but you can hear everything. The breath sounds like a word, a deep resonant word that booms across the Abyss and affects the vibrations of the shapes that are spinning. The breath seems to take shape as it crosses the Abyss, appearing as strings as thin as silk that attach to the shapes and begin to interlink them. The strings of breath connect up all the shapes to make a much bigger, more complex shape: the Metatron Cube.

Once it is complete, it begins to move down the Inner Desert, and each time it reaches a place of power in the Inner Desert, the pattern changes slightly, strengthening and taking a more solid appearance. You walk alongside the pattern, watching it as it spins and moves. Its strong sounds echo around the Inner Desert like a choir of deep

5.12. The vision of the Metatron Cube

harmonies. The Sandalphon walk one on each side of the pattern with the Metatron Cube, to the edge of the Inner Desert up to the area of Malkuth. There the pattern pauses and waits as if for some cue. Without thinking, you look up and see stars moving and shifting, and they also give off a faint sound that joins in with the harmonies in the Inner Desert. The stars seem to reach a certain pattern or constellation and there is a sudden powerful shift, like a door clicking open.

The pattern steps forward with the Sandalphon, crossing over the threshold of Malkuth. The minute the pattern crosses that threshold, it turns into a human form and walks off into the mists of time and physical manifestation. It all happens so quickly, you struggle to understand what it is you have just witnessed. What you have in fact witnessed is the conversion of the utterance of Divinity into form: the creation of Man.

The Inner Desert is silent when the pattern has gone and it holds a strange eerie stillness, as though all the energy of the Inner Desert has just been used up and it has exhaled. This is the 'still point' before the inhalation, when the process will start all over again. The pattern of the Metatron cube is the blueprint for humanity and that blueprint is something you also passed through as your soul stepped out of Divine Being and into the circles of reincarnation. One day, the Inner Desert will inhale and you also will go back to the source, when your times of reincarnations are over. But for now, you savour the stillness of the Inner Desert. It is not the same stillness of the Void, which is a true emptiness: the stillness of the Inner Desert is the pause before action, the taking a second to catch breath after a hard job.

The Sandalphon places a hand upon your shoulder, and tells you it is time to leave. But before you turn to step into the Void, the angel places a thumb upon your forehead and presses hard. It feels like he has made an indent in your forehead to which he puts his lips. He begins to utter strange sounds and words that vibrate through your brain and make you feel strange. The angel is inserting the wisdom and knowledge of the complexity of the pattern that you have just witnessed, so that over the next few years, you will be able to unravel its deepest Mysteries and truly, fully, understand the power that is that pattern.

5. How to work with angels: bound, religious, part human and natural

The angel removes his thumb and pushes you backwards. You fall onto your back and fall through the sand, falling down and down, deeper and deeper into the land and into time. You feel yourself in the pattern, feeling your consciousness linking into a complex weave with angelic beings holding the threads to ensure the pattern is woven carefully. You also feel a feminine force, not a motherly or gentle female power, but a truly awesome, fiery, battle-ready woman who also weaves fate and time. A face flashes before you: that of a woman with a mass of tangled hair, of powerful strong eyes and muscled, battle-scarred arms: a goddess who has truly fought for the survival of humanity and who weaves the fate of the future based on her wisdom and understanding gained in battle.

She touches the threads and you feel her all around you. She makes sounds and the angels holding the threads of the weave move as if in a strange dance. Her face appears and disappears in front of you, and your vision is obscured by fog. The images of her fade deeper and deeper into the mist until you find yourself completely surrounded by mist and dark. It is still, it is dark and it is silent. You feel safe and you feel held. Your mind drifts, allowing your deeper self to take over, a self which remembers this feeling with great comfort, and with great happiness. You drift in the dark small space, completely surrounded by a feeling of love and safety.

A noise awakens you and calls your name. You wake up and step forward but there is nothing beneath your feet for you to stand upon and you fall, turning around and around as if rolling down a hill. You finally uncurl and come to a sudden stop, finding yourself in your body sat before a candle flame. You feel a bit disorientated, as if you came back too quickly, and you want to go back to that safe warm still place. Sit for a while until you are ready to open your eyes. Remember what you have seen, remember the pattern and remember the goddess who wove you. When you are ready, open your eyes and blow out the candle flame.

★ ★ ★

As soon as you have come out of the vision, write down everything you can remember, as it will fade very quickly no matter how strong it is in your mind. Also draw out the pattern, as there will be much for you to retrieve by recreating it. Don't use a ruler but allow your hand to work the pattern from within you.

The experience at the edge of the Abyss will have long and far-reaching ripples of contact if you work a few times with it. It is a deep and powerful working that really takes you to the stripped-down form of angelic power, and truly demonstrates the dynamics of Divinity working with angelic beings to give form to humanity.

The observing of angelic beings at this level gives one a deeper understanding of these beings, and also wipes out any fantasy we may have about angels being soft fluffy handsome blond boys. They are in truth bloody ugly most of the time, and if not ugly, just plain weird.

Another way to observe natural angels in their home setting is to work in the directions with them both ritually and in vision at the same time. Working with the directional elements allows you to see the angelic beings as they express themselves through those elements. A good example of this is a working I did many years ago with a group of magicians while I was living in Bath. The apartment where I lived was over some of the remains of the ancient temple to Sul, Goddess of the hot springs and Underworld. So the room where we were working was a strongly tuned temple extension, and able to handle a great deal of power.

We were working in the directions. I was in the North and one of the adepts was in the south. He was raising angelic power of the South and of fire, and my job was to mediate that out from the center to the west/humanity. He built the power up and then released it: vast swathes of fire emerged out of the south, and out of the flames shot many Wheels of fire spinning at high speed. The Wheels had many eyes that seemed to bore into your soul as they passed you. They circled around the room and then shot out of the window, out into the world. (Bear in mind this was happening in vision, not literally!)

The power and intensity of the contact was massive and really took me by surprise. I was still quite young at the time and had not experienced that level of angelic contact in quite that way before. It changed how I understood angelic contact and it certainly changed the way I approached working with them. In that hour, the adept, who was very skilled and experienced, taught me more about angelic

5. How to work with angels: bound, religious, part human and natural

contact than I could have learned from years of study. That is always the best way to learn, and his ability to mediate and control power to such depth opened my eyes to the level of skill that an adept could reach. He was a wonderful inspiration and has remained one of the people I truly look up to, not only for his skill that he demonstrated that day, in his usual understated way, but for his general humility, sense of honour and wonderful wisdom. I dedicated this book to him to pay respect where respect was due.

If you wish to develop angelic work to that level, I suggest you first work in the visionary scenario of the Inner Desert, to enable your body to get used to the level of power. Once your body can handle that contact, then begin to work in the directions, both ritually and in vision. That will allow you a slow bodily adjustment so that you do not fry yourself.

If you work in magical service to any real level, you will have to work with angelic beings, just as you will have to work with demonic beings, and it is work that will have an impact upon your body one way or another. The only way to minimize that impact to is to grade your body into the power levels slowly. The more humanized or named the angels are, the less of an impact it will have upon your body. As you move further and further away from bound, named or structured angels, the more the body will buckle under the impact. There are countless examples of such impacts in ancient and religious texts: the Old Testament story of Jacob is a good example. He was injured through his interactions with angelic beings, but he also discovered the Ladder of Angels. The Ladder of Angels is a visionary structure in which the hands of angels carry you and pass you from hand to hand up the Abyss to take you to the foot of God. It is a powerful and dangerous process which is used in a variety of ways, including the vision of Justice and Judgement, which is included in my book *The Exorcist's Handbook*. If you decide to work on that vision, make sure you have a very good reason to do so, and that whatever the reason is, you must be prepared to have your life changed forever.

5.13 The Archon and the Aeon

There is an absolute load of twaddle written about the Archon and the Aeon, about what they are, what they do and to whom they answer. They have been dressed in many guises, and married off to various fantasy goddesses or demons or both, usually to fit an agenda of a religion, or to go with the fashion of that magical line.

In reality, when you encounter these beings in vision, they are powerful, and close enough to Divinity to have no real discernible form. These two opposing powers create a tension that works on a variety of levels of consciousness and manifestation. They are the opposing tensions, or polarities, that allow all substance to manifest. They are the alarm system for Divinity, triggered by any human who gets too close to Divinity: their tension creates a threshold that is very close to the source of Divine Universal Power as it manifests in our world.

The Archon and Aeon are hives of consciousness that are part angelic and part Divine. In real terms for us, pushing deep into the Void with the intention of reaching God will eventually bring you face to face with these opposing powers. They snap like an elastic band, literally kicking you out of the Inner Worlds and giving your body a good kicking for good measure. They are the intense light and intense darkness of creation: they are power in and power out, dense and ethereal: they are complete contrasts like two ends of a magnet, never meeting, always dancing around each other. They have no communicable consciousness: you cannot talk to them, and they are just too vast for us. They lie dormant in their opposition until someone reaches a bit too deeply into the inner realms and gets to the threshold of Divinity. At that point their silk thin line of control is disturbed and they contract and react, creating a wave of energy that barrels over anything in its path, snapping you back into your body with a thump and a lot of bruises.

They protect the integrity of Divinity and stop humans from becoming Gods. In our human form, we must not get too close to the reality of Divinity: if we do, we lose our bodies and do not fulfil the purpose of our manifestation in the first place. This is what is just so amazingly wonderful about our world: everything and I mean everything has purpose, power and connection. It is the most

5. How to work with angels: bound, religious, part human and natural

beautiful thing to behold in action, and the Archon and Aeon ensure that it stays that way.

I do not write about them for you to work with; rather, it is important to know these things and to put them in context, so that you get the bigger picture.

5.14 Working advice

In advanced practice, the best way of all to work with any form of angelic being is to be open, simple and straight to the point. You do not need to dress these beings and they do not need long formal ritual wordy prayers or invocations: they do not have egos, so it is pointless brown-nosing them with impressive and gushing compliments. Just call them and tell them why you have called them, or go to them in vision, or both.

At the end of the day, we learn about angels so that we can learn to work with them. Just knowing what they do, what their names are and where they hang out is not enough. There are beings that wish to be worked with, and this is a step closer to a deeper Mystery of all the beings of the earth working together. And we wouldn't really work with them to benefit ourselves: we offer ourselves in service to do things that they cannot. They in turn do the things for us that we cannot do.

The following vision is just one of many examples of how angel and human can work together in service. This vision takes us to the point of death in an individual and we work with the angelic being to assist the passing of this spirit.

5.15 Vision of the pattern of death

Light a candle and close your eyes. With your inner vision see the candle before you. As you look at the candle with your inner vision a peace rises up into you and the stillness descends upon you. You reach deeper down into the earth and you feel the depths of the planet beneath your feet and the height of the stars above your head. The light of the flame burns deep within you.

5.15. Vision of the pattern of death

The flame grows bigger and bigger until all that you can see is fire. Out of the fire steps an angelic being. The angel stands in front of you and reaches out to touch you on the forehead. As soon as they touch your forehead, you fall forward into the angel. The angel allows you to fall through him, and you find yourself falling through the stars with the angel following you.

You fall and fall until you see the planet below you. You fall towards a landmass, a country, a town, a street, a house. You pass through the roof of a house and find yourself in a room where someone is dying on a bed. Someone is sitting with the dying person and in the corner is a man praying and reciting from a holy book. The prayers and recitations appear as many beautiful forms of energy that make a pattern. The pattern has triggered the angel to attend and you are called by the angel to work with them. The man reciting in the corner is not aware that you are there.

The angel touches you on the shoulder and you begin to see in a different way. As you look at the dying person, you start to see in them a beautiful web pattern that is damaged in some areas. In the center of the web, by the person's abdomen, is an orb of light that is glowing dimly. You wonder of it is possible to heal the person. The angel tells you to go forward and touch the person.

You sit by the edge of the bed and you hold the hand of the person who is dying. As you touch them you can feel that the body can no longer hold onto life and that it is time for this spirit to move on. You instinctively reach towards the central orb and pick it up. It breaks the connection with the web and the person breathes their last breath. The angelic being reaches over and assists the spirit to begin to separate from the body. You are told to place the orb where it belongs. You go outside and dig a hole, placing the orb inside the hole. Immediately the orb begins to break up and melt into the earth to be regenerated.

You return to the room and watch as the spirit slowly begins to separate from the body, letting go one by one of the threads that connect it to the body. The spirit listens to the recitation and watches the words as they form into patterns. The patterns tell the spirit which way to go, how to move forward to begin the death journey and what to expect.

5. HOW TO WORK WITH ANGELS: BOUND, RELIGIOUS, PART HUMAN AND NATURAL

A door appears before the spirit and as the door swings open, you feel the power of the Void flow into the room. The Void calls to the spirit and the spirit moves towards the door, drawn by the power and beauty of the Void. Once the spirit has passed through the door and is ready to begin its journey, the door closes. You instinctively go towards the door but the angel holds you back. To step through this door would mean instant death. The angel shows you a wall of fire and you step towards the fire. As you pass into the flames, you feel the fire rebalancing you. You pass through the flames and emerge in the room where you first started. You look at the flame for a second before gently blowing it out.

★ ★ ★

If you wished to take that work further, and walk with the person through death, to be of assistance, then instead of walking through the door, you would go into the Underworld and find the River of Death. You would follow the river until it opens out in the Inner Desert. From there, you can work safely, talking to the person and when they are ready, suggesting to them that they cross the bridge over the river and walk deeper into death.

Finally, if you are going to work in any depth with angels, get fit and look after your body because they are the ones more than any other being you will encounter that will knock the shit out of your body. You will get bruised, dislocated and even fractured if you are not careful. And always be straight to the point. If you make a mistake or are vague with your intentions, you may end up with something that you really did not want to happen.

Chapter Six

Practical methods for creating ritual tools

There are many ways levels and methods of working with the consecration of ritual tools and in the early phases of magical training, learning how to attune or enliven an implement is the foundation for more powerful consecrations and object mediations. Once a magician has learned to tune in a tool, then the next step is to consecrate the tool to tune it to the 'original': there is only ever one consecrated sword for example, and all ritual swords are a part of it, like a hive consciousness. In this section we will look at the technique of consecrating a ritual implement, and we will also look at putting beings/workers/powers into tools specifically for a job, after which they are taken out again. The tool becomes a vessel for a coworker that brings a specific quality with it. We will also look at awakening Divinity within a tool.

6.1 Consecration of tools in the deepest part of the temple

This method of consecration basically cuts out a lot of the middlemen—the priesthoods who often have agendas—and goes straight to the 'source' of the angelic threshold. This action leapfrogs all of the generations upon generations of magical/priesthood layers with all of their attendant degeneracy. Going back to the source also takes the implement back to the very first expression of the original consecrated and sacred implement, which often has its roots deeply embedded within the sacred land.

As with all true consecrations, you cannot dictate exactly what is going to go into the tool; and although you may start in a traditional

6. Practical methods for creating ritual tools

direction for that tool, you must be willing to be flexible if the tool decides that actually its consecration line needs to come from a completely different direction.

When you decide you want to properly consecrate a ritual implement, you must first be willing to think it through and be aware of all the responsibilities and consequences of such an action. Unlike an attuned tool, a consecrated tool will last forever, and if it is broken up, it is possible that its power will remain in its fragments. They are very difficult to destroy and can be dangerous to keep, depending on what power is in them and how will have access to them. Also bear in mind that a fully consecrated sword, for example, is a very dangerous and powerful tool that can weak havoc on a home, community or even land if wielded without knowledge and wisdom. So what will happen to it once you have died/given up magic/become a politician? You need to make proper plans for the tool to ensure its guardianship after you have gone. That is the whole point of the story of Excalibur: the dying king commands that the sword be returned to the water where it will be safe from the hands of men. It must be buried, or put in water, or burned and returned to its source. If you bury it or cast it into water, then you must also charge an angelic guardian to watch over it and keep people away from it.

Seeing as we are on the theme of swords, we shall look at the consecration method for a ritual sword. For the other implements, depending on what element/direction they want to work in, you would simply adjust the direction/element in the vision.

The following consecration vision and ritual places the power of the wind in the sword, which is the power of utterance and justice. This would be worked with in the east. If the sword were to be consecrated to be a sword of protection, say for a landmass, then you would work with the volcanic power in the south. If it was to be a sword of sovereignty, then it would be worked with in the north.

6.2 Consecration ritual/vision for a consecrated Sword of Justice

Set the ritual working space up with an altar in the center and an altar in the east. On each altar is a candle, and the altar in the east should

6.2. Consecration ritual/vision for a consecrated Sword of Justice

have a small dish of consecrated oil and nothing else. By the door have a pad of paper and a pen in case you have to write something down.

The sword should be prepared the night before by placing it in a sheet or cloth that is filled with dry salt: leave it wrapped in the salt. In the morning, the sword is washed, dried and exposed to the outside air briefly. Ensure that you are also prepared which means that you must take a consecrated bath the morning of the work and wear clothing that has no script, words or faces upon it: Plain clothes or robes, and no jewellery unless it is ritual jewellery.

Take the sword and place it upon the central altar. Light the candle and be in the stillness, use your inner flame to light the inner candle and stand for a moment in silence to give the room time to tune in properly. Then go and light the flame on the altar in the east. Remember to process around all four directions before you get to the east, to strengthen and continue the tide of power that swirls in the room like a whirlpool. Light the candle in the east and be still and silent as the flame tunes itself. Once the direction is tuned, then you must open the gates of the east. Place a hand on either side of the candle and close your eyes, see with your mind's eye the two gates slowly swinging open, and you will see a passageway that vanishes off into the mist. See yourself stepping over the threshold and into the east. You walk into the mist with the intention of reaching for the deepest part of the power of air and angelic justice. As you walk in the mist a wind begins to blow, and as you walk deeper and deeper into the mist the wind becomes stronger. The mist vanishes and you find yourself trying to walk along a passageway that is slightly banked up a slope with a strong wind blowing directly at you from somewhere.

The wind becomes so strong that you can barely stand up, and you find yourself crawling up the slope to reach a pair of doors that the wind seems to be blowing out of. Inch by inch you crawl against the wind until you reach the great doors. The wind is blowing through the keyhole and you realize that if you open the doors, there is a very good chance that you will be destroyed by the wind. But you know it is something that must be done, not only for the work, but also for your own development. Your hands grasp the door handles and with every ounce of strength you have, you pull upon the doors to open them. A terrible wind screams out from the crack of the opening

6. Practical Methods for Creating Ritual Tools

doors and it blows you over. And then the wind falls and you lie on the floor surrounded by the most beautiful scent of flowers.

You sit up and before you, beyond the great doors to the inner sanctum, is a whirlwind spinning at great speed. Its wind has eyes looking in all directions. The whirlwind gives off a deep rumbling sound and a faint but beautiful light. The wind that floats slowly from the fast spinning center is scented with the smell of wildflowers: the smell grips your heart in a clutch of long-forgotten memories that rise in your mind. Now that you have opened the great inner sanctum, it is time to get the sword and take it into the angelic wind for consecration. In your mind you return to the altar where you are stood and you walk clockwise to the sword that is waiting on the centre altar.

First the sword must be ritually stripped of anything that is in it, so that it is a blank slate, ready for the power that is about to be placed within it. The following is done in vision and also ritually, which your physical voice. Where you see +, it means mark an equal-armed cross in the air over the object. With your left hand, hold the hilt of the sword, and with your right hand, pointing the first two fingers at the blade, recite: "I exorcize you, creature of the Earth by the living gods + the Holy Gods + the omnipotent Gods + that thou mayst be purified of all evil influence in the name of Adonai, lord of all angels and men." The power of the wind flows through your voice and you feel a great power mediating through you as you speak. Pass the blade of the sword through the candle flame and in your mind's eye, see the flames consume the blade and cleanse it. The second half of that recitation will come after the vision.

Take the sword from the centre and walk a full clockwise circle around the directions, finishing in front of the altar in the east. Close your eyes and, holding the sword in your hands, step over the threshold and into the passageway that leads to the whirlwind. This time there is no heavy wind, just the mild breeze with the scent of flowers that blows gently around you as you walk up to the inner sanctum. As you reach the threshold, you bow to the power of Divinity manifest in the whirlwind, and you also physically bow, even though you are working in vision. See yourself step over the threshold and approach the whirlwind, whose many eyes have all trained themselves upon you. They search within you, they see every

6.2. Consecration ritual/vision for a consecrated Sword of Justice

part of you, and they see all of your intentions. This is the angel of Justice in its deepest form: the whirlwind that sees all. You are prompted to hold out the sword, which is instantly whipped out of your hand and absorbed by the wind. The sword is changed from an inner perspective before being released by the wind and dropped at your feet.

You are told to turn your back to the wind and to hold the sword out before you, the point facing down to the floor. Behind you, out of the whirlwind, steps an angelic being that places its hands upon your shoulders. The angel puts its face to the back of your neck and begins to blow into you. A pressure builds up within you, filling your lungs and your mind. The angel begins to speak into the base of your neck and your mouth is forced open. Out of your mouth come sounds, but as you breathe them over the sword, you see the sounds taking shape and becoming sigils that mark the blade. You must concentrate and remember as many of them as you can: they are the angelic keys to the power that has been placed within the sword. Once the angel has finished, it grasps your hair and tells you to recite. You do the recitation in vision and physically with your voice. Holding the sword in one hand, you place your right hand with the flat of its palm up to the sword, and recite the following: "creature of the earth and the wind, I consecrate thee in the name of (-) to the service of the Gods and Goddesses." (The G-D name that you use depends on what powers you work with and in what tradition you are working. Alternatively you can utter simply Divine Being.)

Mark one of the sigils that you saw with your index finger onto the blade both in vision and physically. When you do it physically, dip your index finger into the oil and mark the sigil by the hilt. Back away from the inner sanctum, bow and return to the threshold. See yourself once more stood at the altar with the sword, take a step back and bow once more, thanking the inner contacts, guardians and angelic beings for working with you. Take the sword all around the four directions even though they are not lit and hold it up, hilt up, in each direction as an acknowledgement before finally putting it by the central candle. See the central flame, which is the flame that burns at the edge of the Void, flow into the sword, giving it life. The flame sits within the sword and finishes the enlivening. Every time you pick up the sword, you must be aware of that flame of life within

6. Practical Methods for Creating Ritual Tools

it, the sigils which are the angelic keys to its knowledge upon it, and of the responsibility the holder carries.

Go out of the room while leaving the candles burning. It may take an hour or so for the inner ritual to complete itself, and you will feel when it is finished. When you feel that completion, go back in and starting at the east altar, thank the contacts, close the gates and blow the flame back into the Void. Do the same with the central flame and wrap or scabbard the sword, leaving it in the east of the sacred space.

The next step will be the enlivening of the scabbard. As soon as you can, get the pen and paper and write the sigils that you remember.

* * *

The consecration method above reaches beyond human consecration lines, reaching instead for the angelic thresholds of power that flow through people and objects. Because it is a deep consecration method, you must understand that you will be held responsible for the inner and outer health of the sword, for its power will be strong and potentially dangerous. Do not let anyone other than you touch it: you birthed its power through mediation and it will be specifically tuned therefore to work with your power structure only. If someone else tried to handle it or use it for magic it could potentially be very destructive.

The basic structure of the above ritual works for any direction and any quality of the direction for any of the implements. What changes in the four directions is the elemental expression. Notice that there was no landscape, elaborate temple etc., just the pure power of the element beyond the gates and the angelic mediator. When you tune to the pure element of the direction, the angelic contact will appear to mediate it to and through you once it has figured out what you are actually trying to do. If the element does not respond to you, speak across the element, telling it what you are trying to achieve, and then the angelic contact should emerge out of the element. They may appear as human, non-human or just downright weird.

Just an aside: if you are working in the east, try not to do it in the spring, as there is a good chance, depending on what landmass you are on, that ritually opening the gates to the depths of the east wind may cause a very large burp of tornadoes or lightning storms. You will very probably end up in one of those 'oops' moments. You will need to spend some time working with the sword to find out exactly what power is flowing through specifically and how that power works with you. Just tread very carefully until you have a good idea about what it actually can do.

6.3 Ritually enlivening the scabbard

The scabbard contains and completes the power of the sword, bringing it ballast and ancestral connection. It is not just a holder, but a nurturer, teacher and stabilizer. Without a proper scabbard, a sword can become feral, can become distorted and often become unwieldy. Magicians who do not have enlivened scabbards for their swords often, over the years, become aggressive in their magic and develop the tendency to curse people. The power needs a proper containment and the scabbard is a power that anchors the destructive energy within the sword, ensuring that its powers are always directed in work and not left hanging about, which enables that destructive power to seep into the magician's everyday life.

If the sword did not come with a scabbard, then you will need to get one made or make one yourself. It should have no sigils, shapes, words or pictures upon it, just plain leather or cloth. Patterns that are decorative are fine as long as no beings are represented.

Set up the sacred space with just the central altar and the altar in the north. As before, strip the scabbard and cleanse it with salt, and have sacred oil on the altar in the north. Light the central candle and tune it to the flame in the Void and the flame within you, and then light the candle in the north. See the gates of the north open as you stand there in the stillness and beyond the gates, you see mist.

Take the scabbard to the altar in the north and place it upon the altar. In vision, with your hands still upon the scabbard, step over the threshold and into the mists. You will find yourself walking among large standings stones that loom out of the mist and one of them you notice is covered in many intricate patterns. Before the stone is a well, and you find yourself peering down the well. Something shoves you from behind, and clutching onto the scabbard, you find yourself falling through water, down and down into the depths of the earth. You fall through the water, into the deep dark earth, clutching the scabbard to you as you fall. You fall and fall until the light of the world you have fallen from fades away and you are left to fall in darkness.

You land with a bump on a soft floor and find yourself standing before a rough-hewn rock doorway with a faint light glowing beyond it. You push open the door, which is made of a very strong, almost metallic wood that is the deepest black you have ever seen.

Beyond the door you find yourself in a cave that is lit by a faint green light emitting from its walls. On the floor are many sleeping creatures and birds, and at the other end of the cave you see an old woman sat on a stone throne. She is slumped over a hound that is on her lap, and she seems to be sleeping. The dog opens one eye to look at you and begins to growl quietly. The old lady begins to awaken, and as she sits up, she looks at you. Her face is a mass of wrinkles, her hair, long and grey-white, but her eyes have the youth of a woman in her prime. They are bright, powerful and see right through you. She looks at the scabbard and nods to herself before beckoning you to approach her. She reaches out her hand and asks for the scabbard. When you give her the scabbard, she also asks for whatever is in your pocket. Reach in to your pocket and whatever you see there, you give to her. If it is something that you own in life, then you must give it away to a stranger or bury it. If it is something big, like your house, you must let it go and be willing to let it go in real life...learn to trust.

The old woman takes a thread of her hair and begins to weave. She takes hair from the hound, moss from the walls, hair from her body and hair and feathers from the animals and birds around her. She weaves and weaves until they are all woven into the scabbard and then she spits on it to smooth it down. She then pricks her finger and lets a drop of blood fall onto the weave. You also do the same (and physically, prick your finger and drop the blood onto the scabbard).

She then hugs the scabbard to her and tells you that you have to get it from her. Think very very carefully about how you approach this and how you get her to give up the scabbard. Once you have got the scabbard from her you hold it up to look at the weave and you see a pair of eyes looking back at you: her bright sharp eyes have been woven into the scabbard, and as you look back at her, you see that her eyes are missing. She will be within the scabbard, being the eyes of the sword and protecting it as it rests. You realize that a part of this being is now in the scabbard and you must treat it accordingly with respect and reverence. The scabbard is the more powerful of the two, and guides, aims, advises and protects the sword. Carefully you carry the scabbard up a long stone stairway that the scabbard guides you to, and you climb slowly through the Underworld, reaching for the surface world above you. The scabbard is not a tool, it is an inner contact from deep within the earth, a fragment of the ancient Goddess and you must remember that at all times.

You emerge by the threshold of the altar and you step back into yourself, finding yourself stood before the flame, the scabbard in your hands. Open your eyes and look at the flame. Look at the scabbard and thank the sacrifice that the contact has made to be there for you and to guide you. The contact within the scabbard will teach you many magical things about the sword, the scabbard and the Underworld if you are willing to listen and learn. Place your right hand upon the scabbard and recite: "I vow to uphold your honour, to work with you wisely, to listen to your guidance and to tend to your needs. Thank you Great Goddess, for the gift of your eyes." Bow to the flame, to give honour to the sacredness of the being within the scabbard and the Divine Power within the flame.

Blow out the flame, sending it back into the Void, and then circle the directions before placing the scabbard by the central flame. You will need to immediately paint two eyes onto the scabbard while the candle flame is still burning. Once the eyes are finished, leave the room with the candle still going and let the process continue until you feel it complete. Once everything has gone silent and the energies have subsided, go back in with the consecrated sword. Place the sword on the altar beside the scabbard and place a hand upon the scabbard and a hand upon the sword. Ask the being that is now the scabbard if they are willing to work with the consecrated sword and be the scabbard for that sword. You will slowly begin to feel the guardian being that is the scabbard looking into the sword and feeling what sort of consecration it has had. You may find questions bubble

6. PRACTICAL METHODS FOR CREATING RITUAL TOOLS

up in your mind, and if that happens, you must answer honestly. These questions are coming into your mind from the scabbard.

Once everyone seems happy with everyone (and if not, then you are well and truly screwed) place the sword in the scabbard and place it on the altar. Go out again for around fifteen minutes or so to let the two settle together while the sacred flame is in attendance. Once all is done, go back in again (ever felt like you are on a piece of elastic?) send the flame back into the Void and gather up the sword which should now, in its scabbard, be kept somewhere, either in the sacred space, or in a place where it can watch over the house/temple. It must not be touched by anyone but you and it must never, ever be unsheathed for any reason other than magical. Do not let people play with it or be curious around it. Such interference will unbalance the sword which could in turn affect your magical work. It could also be dangerous for the various beings and deities in the room.

I once had a situation where a magician thought it would be great to swing around my sword, when I was out of the room, a sword which was a fully contacted consecrated sword with a being in it. Swinging it around the space he managed to break the links to all the guardians of the space, and decapitate the shell that held an ancient demonic being that I was working with...which really pissed them and me off. He undid a year's work in ten minutes. Great. Needless to say he was demoted to dishwasher. If the sword is holding a being, which we will go on to next, untold damage can be done by a curious idiot unsheathing it and playing with it. Simply pointing it at a person and uttering words, even in jest, can result in a lot of very nasty things. These are not playthings, they are not the sort of thing you can buy in a New Age store that looks all magical and has nothing in it. These are powerful, dangerous and productive working tools that are akin to Exocet missiles. Think carefully about where you place them. I found that hanging them on the wall, blade down, is the best: it's not so easy for someone to reach up and take them down. Morons tend to pick up things that are directly in front of them.

When you do work magically with your sword, ensure that you remember that the sword is a tool, but the scabbard is a being (or a window for a being, but you treat it as a direct being). Always be respectful of the scabbard: they are always 'her.' The scabbard is a fragment of the Dark Goddess of the cave: this is where the sword and the stone comes from. The sword sleeps in the sacred element of earth/ land, and the Goddess in the Cave is the Mother of the land. Talk to the scabbard, learn to build up a communion with her so that she can tell you things, warn you of things and advise/teach you. If you use the sword in vision or ritual, tell the scabbard first, let her prepare for the work and when you unsheathe the sword, place the scabbard on the altar and she will work with you as a coworker. Eventually she will begin to show you herself in vision as woman, and you will be able to build up a communion with her as an inner contact.

6.4 Placing a being within the sword

This is another way of working with magical tools that can be used for any of the tools be they sword, wand, cup or shield. Instead of consecrating the tools, they become vessels for beings that are heavily linked into the element and direction you are working with. Or they can be linked into specific powers that you need to work with for a length of time. The beings can either be brought into take up permanent residence, or they can be brought in for a particular length of service, even just for one vision, and then returned to their source. Just remember if you have a being in a tool permanently or for a long while, then they will need some upkeep and a wary eye keeping on them.

This is a very powerful way of working with a sword, and a magician would use this technique if there is a very heavy or prolonged and dangerous piece of work to do. The same is true of all the other directional tools.

The first thing to remember with this kind of work is that there is an outer tool and an inner tool and you have to work with both. There is a method for putting a being directly into a tool but I have found by experience that this is not always the best way to work: they get bored, hungry and sometimes feral. It is better to create a bridge to the being from both the inner and outer tool so that the tool becomes an extension of the being, rather than the being itself. So when you work with the tool, the being will be alerted and will be aware of you

6. Practical methods for creating ritual tools

and will work with you, but when the tool is not in use, the being will not be there. It's a bit like leaving the phone line open.

6.5 Bridging a being into a tool

Firstly you need to ascertain which direction the being you wish to work with is residing in, or if they are in a landscape, historical place, etc. If they are in a direction, then you can work with the altar in that direction as an anchor and threshold. If the being is in the Underworld, overworld, the past or in the land around you, then work with the central flame and the central altar.

Essentially, you go in vision to the being, wherever it may be, and ask the being if it is willing to work with you through this tool. You have the inner tool with you and your physical hand on the physical tool. First the being ties a lock of their hair, or some of their blood to the tool or will pass into and through the inner tool to make the bridge and connect with it. Once that is done, then tie a lock of the being's hair to a lock of your hair or to your wrist if you have no hair, and walk out of the vision back to the altar with the being connected to you.

Once you return to the altar, place your hands upon the outer tool and invite the being into the tool. It will pass through your body and into the tool. Don't rush this part of the work: give the being time to do the transfer and you will feel when it is completed. When it is finished, when you look with your inner vision, you will see the being within the tool and you will see an umbilical flowing from the tool back into the direction or landscape where you were working.

Leave the tool with the flame for a little while, just to let the being settle in. When it is finished, put out the light and place the tool in its resting place, away from curious hands and eyes. Whenever you work with the tool, see the umbilicus vanishing into the Inner Worlds and see the being within the tool. The more you work and commune with the being, the stronger the bridging will become.

If for example you wished to use the above method for bridging power into a tool for a specific working or task then you would follow the same basic steps. Inner tool, outer tool, go to contact, either give the tool to the contact or have the contact connect themselves to the inner tool. Then bring out the inner tool with the being connected and link them up or put them into the outer tool. Then forge the inner and outer tools together again. A good working action like this is to work with the Fire Temple volcanic sword maker. This contact is mentioned in the chapter of volcanic Fire Temple work, and the contact is a very ancient consciousness that forges metal magical weapons in the depths of volcanoes.

A word of advice, though: whenever you intend to work with the magical tools of sword, wand, cup and shield, do not allow yourself to be influenced by writings or 'truths' about the role, power and wielding of magical tools. Let them be themselves, allow them space to speak to you, to show you who they really are and what they really do...you will be very surprised about what can surface if you do not lay preconceived ideas upon them. There are some interesting writings out there, true, but there is also a pile of bullshit out there that will potentially block you from achieving what it is you want to achieve.

If you want to learn more about a particular magical tool, then work with it, talk to it, go into the Inner Library and ask about it. Once you have been told a few things and shown a few things, then it is time to go and search the outer world for information. That way, when you see something that correlates to what you were told by inner contacts, then you know you are on the right path.

6.6 Awakening Divinity in substance

This is a very different way of working with the magical implements and is best only done if you are working purely from a standpoint of service. If you use this technique for your own ends it simply will just not work. If you are working in service, though, it can be an extremely powerful way of working and will most certainly teach you a lot and mature you a lot as a human spirit.

This technique does not put anything into the tools: rather it awakens to a conscious level the Divinity that is within all substance. The flame of Divine Being in all things is usually an unconscious thread of power, a fragment of the whole and an echo of all creation. If that fragment is awakened and tuned, it becomes a direct interface

6. Practical Methods for Creating Ritual Tools

between the power of Divinity and the magician. The fragment of Divinity within the substance is awakened specifically to the power and consciousness of the magical implement, so the power within the tool is not like an icon of Divine Being that you can talk to or interact with as a humanlike form; rather it is a conscious fragment that is awakened specifically to the power frequency that the tool holds.

The power that awakens within a tool cannot be preempted: it will be individual and purely of itself. How Divinity chooses to express itself through that tool is a Mystery that you will have to unfold slowly yourself. Because of that, I would not recommend using the tool magically straightaway; rather I would suggest spending time with the tool, getting to know its expression, its power and its abilities. It may take years to fully understand exactly what power is in the tool and also, more importantly, what its purpose is. Every Divinely awakened tool has a specific function and you will be held responsible for ensuring that it fulfils its function. Because of this specific way of dealing with the tool, I would only recommend this form of working with magical implements if you had a specific idea of a long-term span of work that was of service: in those circumstances the Divine Tool will work with you in service, and you will learn its powers and skills as the work unfolds.

The preparation for such awakening begins with the acquisition of the tool. It must be virgin, i.e. never used before for magic, and preferably a brand new tool, a newly forged sword, a branch taken from a tree, a newly made cup and a handmade or newly made shield or a stone that you have found yourself. You would not salt it, as you do not want to strip out everything within it: you want to awaken the latent power within it. That will mean that you awaken not only the divine power within the object, but also the inner spirit of the element, or tree, or rock. The skill that is needed to do this job is stillness, total and complete inner stillness.

To begin, light a candle in the centre and sit in a chair before the altar with the tool in your hand. Close your eyes and see the inner flame with your inner vision. You find yourself drawn more and more to the flame, and find yourself passing into the flame, bathing in its regenerative life power. The flames fill you up, filling you with a sense of peace and stability. You find yourself stepping through the flame and emerging out into the Void, into the place where there is no time,

6.6. Awakening Divinity in substance

no space and no movement. You spread out, no longer restricted by a body, allowing your spirit to flow freely in all directions at once. You become aware of a vastness within you, of the Void within and you also become aware of the tool that is in your hands as your body sits before a flame.

In the Void you hold the inner pattern of the tool in your hand and you begin to push deeper into the nothing, moving further and further into the Void and away from the physical world. As you push deeper and deeper into the Void, your memory of the physical world falls away and you find yourself merging with the Void, with a deep sense of belonging and of coming home. You begin to remember the feeling of this place: you have spent much time here, during lives and between lives: it is your home, your place of rest and regeneration. You push deeper and deeper into the Void until you find a very narrow path before you. Something tells you that you must collect yourself together, to take human form again, and walk this narrow path.

With the tool in your hand, you walk the narrow ledge through the Void, walking through nothing and yet feeling a great deal around you. The ledge comes to an end, beyond which is a nothing that feels completely empty and very different from the Void around you. The hair on your neck starts to prickle and you feel a massive amount of power building up around you. The air around you becomes very pressured and it gets hard to breathe properly. The tool in your hand begins to vibrate with the change of frequencies and out of the depths of the Void comes a wave of pressure that washes over you.

From that wave merges a being with many eyes, many wings and is made up of strange shapes. The being touches you upon the forehead with a touch that seems to light up your brain. The being then places a hand over the tool and grasps it tight. You watch as the tool changes and you begin to see all the molecules that make up the substance of the tool. Each molecule sparks brightly with life, and when all the molecules are bright, a surge of power flows through the being and into the tool. The tool begins to pulsate with life and energy and it weighs heavy in your hand. The angel turns and vanishes back into the Void and you are told to leave. You walk back along the ledge, the tool getting heavier and heavier as you walk. By the time

6. Practical Methods for Creating Ritual Tools

you come to the part of the Void where you first started, the tool is so heavy you can barely lift it.

You remember the flame that you were seated before and with that memory you step out of the Void, through the flame and back into the room where you first started. The tool is very heavy and you place it on the altar with the candle flame and leave the room. You leave the tool with the candle until you feel it is time to go in and put the candle out. From now on, whenever you are going to use the tool, first light a candle before it and leave it for a few minutes before the stillness of the flame. When the tool is not in use, wrap it in a cloth or put it in a box away from prying eyes and curious fingers.

6.7 Summary

The methods of creating, maintaining and using magical implements are endless and really depend of what you are doing, where you are doing it and why. The main thing to remember is, at the end of the day, you will gain more from working with tools using methods gleaned from your own inner work and from sources that you have been guided to. There are many very powerful ways to work with magical tools and the old rule, which always applies, is 'when you need a tool, it will appear': you just need to keep your eyes open and realize what has just dropped on your doorstep.

Have the tools hang out with you while you work, that way you will be able to bridge into the consciousness of the tool and learn about it as you work. In truth, the deeper and more powerful the magic that you work with, the less you have to do anything specific with the tools: they just stay in the working space and do their job quietly. Just don't let the neighbours kids grab them and play with them, it leaves such a mess on the carpet.

Chapter Seven

The magic of the Underworld

In my opinion, the Underworld and all its beings, deities, sub-realms and landscapes should be the first training ground for all magicians, but sadly this area of magic is often left until the magician is already an adept. The Underworld teaches us about our past, our ancestors, and the distant past of the planet; it shows us about death and gives us access to the powers and landscapes of death; and it is the home of the ancient Mother Goddess, along with many strange-looking ancient beings. Very old shamanic magic sinks into the Underworld once it has been abandoned, and to touch base and learn about this vast array of ancient knowledge should be a priority for all magicians and priest/esses.

The back door of the Underworld is the Abyss, i.e. the place where the consciousness of the Underworld resides without the dressing of the manifest world. Every realm has a front door and a back door, and once the Underworld has been explored and learned about by going into the earth, then it is time for the magician to explore and work in the depths of the Abyss. To access the deep parts of the Abyss without first having experience of the Underworld as it manifests in our world (which is the death realm and ancestral realm, containing Titans and massive Underworld Goddess Temples, etc.) is suicide: it's that simple.

The backroom of the universe, which is the Abyss, does not have all the inherent safety valves built into it that the Underworld does so it is far easier to get eaten by an ancient being while you are down the Abyss than it is in the Underworld. In this chapter, we will briefly look at some of the various realms in the Underworld, and then we will look into the deep part of the Abyss to see how it all hangs together. The two previous books in this series do touch upon various Underworld realms, i.e. the death realm, ancestors etc., and

7. THE MAGIC OF THE UNDERWORLD

you will find a few Underworld contacts and connections scattered around this book in other chapters. If you bring them all together, you will find a map of the Underworld.

When we go down into the earth below our feet we first hit the faery realm, which is also entwined with the surface world, then we hit our ancestors buried within the earth. In a visionary sense, one of the very first visions we find in the earth, usually in a cave, is an Underworld Goddess who presents as an old woman living in a cave with a pool of water. This image is found all across the Northern hemisphere from India to England. She is our first contact with the female consciousness of the land. As we dig deeper, we start to find older deities that have vanished from our world, the River of Death, sleepers from the ancient past, ancient temples from thousands of years ago, and then below them very large beings known as the old gods or titans.

Around that layer of Underworld consciousness we come across very ancient forms of humanity who still work as inner contacts, mediating Underworld power to the surface world and working with the raw forces of Divinity as they express through nature. Their power often brings destruction to our world, in a cleaning way, but more often than not their bridge to the surface world is blocked by ritual seals and locked doors placed there by some of the early monotheistic religions and some of the Classical religions who manipulated the deities to suit themselves. Greece and Rome were particularly guilty of such actions.

An adept has a great many reasons to work in the Underworld, not only in a learning capacity, but also in a line of service. The Underworld processes all that has passed, all that will sleep, all that has died, and all that no longer has a place in our world. Those processes take a great deal of mediating and bridging: sleepers need attending to and guarding, magically trapped deities that still have a place in our world need to be released and the land needs help to breathe after all the building we have done upon her. And that is just the outer face of the Underworld. The harder and more dangerous service is often undertaken deep within the Abyss, where beings must be guarded, put back to sleep, honoured, fed and consulted where necessary.

Providing you have worked in the faery realm, the death visions, and the ancestral realm, and you have struck up a suitable relationship with the Goddess in the Cave, then it is time to go a little deeper. The first step would be to visit and work with the Goddess in the Cave as an adept and then the Sisters at the back of the North Wind.

The Goddess in the Cave is a contact that is worked with a lot in the early days of one's visionary training, and she has been a foundational visionary contact in many esoteric and religious mystical practices for millennia. The contact becomes stronger and more profound as our experience grows, and it is one of the basic visions that I feel cannot be reiterated enough, hence I am going to put a visionary version of her in this book, even though she is in my other magical books.

As an initiate, we experience her as a guardian to the gates of the Underworld, as a healer and as a teacher. Once we have progressed in our magical training and we are coming to a path of service, then our relationship with this deity changes. We begin to see the deeper and more profound element to this goddess and work with her in our service to the land and to humanity.

There are certain details that should be observed when working in this realm, for instance, how the cave appears, which beings are in there sleeping with her, what she looks like, what attendants she has (if any), what state the pool is in, and whether she is armed or not. The cave is a threshold place in the Underworld and it is a space where the past and future collide: octaves are layered upon each other so when something is coming in the nearer future that is an echo of an ancient past, it will affect how the cave presents itself. If there are no animals or birds in there, it is because these animals are soon going to be extinct or at least removed off the landmass that her cave serves. How everything presents will tell you the health of the land, what is coming and also will hint about what your work will be. It can also be a place where the newly dead appear if they are connected to her in some way or other.

She can be worked with as an oracle for the near future of the land and civilization, and she can also help in cleaning up a heavily parasited person or place: she will give you tools, advice and helpers

7. The magic of the Underworld

should you need them. She is a major advisor for magicians working in the Underworld, and will also offer some protection if she deems it necessary. She will also provide foundations for Underworld temples and furnish them with guardians. There is much to be learned from this most ancient of Goddesses and her power should never be underestimated. Her deepest version, which is found in the Abyss, is as a warrior lion goddess who is part human and partly divine: she keeps the balance in all things through destruction, justice and compassion.

The following vision takes you to her in the cave, and it also takes you through the back door into the Abyss where you can follow her work more closely. Be very aware that any gift that you give her in vision must also be given to her in real life: she is a demanding goddess and her effect upon your life can be very real, so do not shortchange her or you will regret it. It is a long vision, and establishes a connection between our world, the Underworld, the Abyss, the Inner Desert and the Void. It is a loop that can only be done by humanity but serves to open doorways for many powers and beings to flow through. Just doing the vision is in itself a major service, but also much can be learned from it and a strong relationship with this goddess can be developed through this work.

7.1 Vision of the Goddess in the Cave and her presence in the Abyss

Light a candle and close your eyes. See the candle with your inner vision and feel the stillness of the Void within the candle flame and within you. As you bathe in the stillness, a hole opens up in the earth and the candle flame falls down into the Underworld, and you follow. The candle flame lights the way ahead as you fall through darkness, falling past rocks, earth, and tree roots until you come to a small cave with a floor of soft sand. You fall onto the sand and the flame falls beside you. As you look around you see an ancient stone stairway leading up to the surface world, a stairway that twists around the directions and that is carved into the rock face. On the other side of the cave an entrance is roughly cut into the stone with a curtain of wool pulled across it. On the curtain are hung many pieces of

7.1. Vision of the Goddess in the Cave and her presence in the Abyss

jewellery: gifts for the goddess. You stand up and walk to the curtain. Carefully you pull it to one side. The cave beyond is dark, and you can hear snoring. Being very quiet, scoop up the flame and hold it in your hand as you tiptoe into the cave: the flame lights the way and also brings stillness to the Underworld.

In the larger cave are many creatures, all fast asleep on the floor. Up around you hang bats, alongside them are perched birds and lizards, all asleep. At the far end of the cave you see an old woman asleep on a stone throne. Her long grey hair has grown into the floor, and her body seems to be joining with the stone chair upon which she is seated. Among her clothing sleep tiny birds and other creatures, and at her feet is curled a large hound. The hound opens one eye and looks at you. This alerts the ancient Goddess, who wakes up, and also looks at you with one eye.

Kneel before her and offer her whatever you find in your pocket. She will either take the gift or tell you to leave. If she takes the gift, tell her that you are learning about the deeper parts of the Underworld so that you can be a better magician. She may ask you questions and she may ask you to do a job for her. If you agree to what she asks you, it is really important that you actually follow through and do what she asks. If it is something you are not comfortable with doing, then you must be honest and say so.

Once that is over, ask her if she will allow you to explore her cave in more depth and if she will allow you to learn about the deeper side of her in the Abyss. If she agrees, stand and bow to her before leaving her. You will find that behind her chair there is a narrow passageway. If she allows you, go down the passageway, taking the flame with you. You will also notice that the hound has properly awoken and is following you: he will ensure your safety as you draw near to the Abyss.

The passageway, which is hewn out of the rock, is roughly decorated with paintings of animals and birds, many of which you have never seen before. These are the memories of creatures that have become extinct and now are only memories, deep in the Underworld. The deeper into the passageway you go, the stranger the animal paintings get, until you realize you are looking at a creative version of dinosaurs. The passageway becomes narrower and you begin to

7. THE MAGIC OF THE UNDERWORLD

notice strange magical symbols on the walls, roof and floor. As you pass over and under them, you feel a strange sensation, almost like cobwebs touching you. These are magical barriers that create a wall between the Underworld and the Abyss: beings must not be able to pass freely from the Abyss to the Underworld. The sense of cobwebs becomes stronger and you begin to feel that you are pushing through some sort of sticky substance in order to continue on your journey. The flame draws closer to you, and the hound is now at your leg, growling softly. The darkness becomes more intense and the air takes on a very distinctive smell that you recognize from somewhere but cannot remember where: you do, however, remember the fear that goes with that smell, and all your defences are on full alert.

The passageway ends at a large and ornate doorway that is guarded by two very large and very strange-looking angelic beings. They have many wings that are wrapped closed around them and a body of many eyes, one of which opens to look at you. They look into your eyes, into your mind and into your soul. They see that you are a magician and that you mean no ill will. One of the angelic beings, either the one on the right or the one on the left, will reach out and mark you upon the forehead, so that you will be identified to other guardians. Whichever side the angel is on when you are touched will indicate a path that has now been finished for you magically. You can enter the Abyss from the Underworld, but you must not try to enter the Underworld from the Abyss: to do so would open a pathway for other beings and could lead to ancient beings finding their way back to our world when they should not.

The angels open the doorway slowly and a puff of stale air greets you. You find yourself in yet another passageway, also decorated with magical symbols designed to stop anyone from wandering through the tunnel and finding their way to the Underworld from the Abyss. The flame stays close to you, but the hound will not cross the threshold into the Abyss: he barks and then turns to go back to his mistress in the cave. The passageway widens a little and you notice paintings that tell stories on the walls. You stop to look at them closer. They are very beautiful, but they do not seem to make much sense to you. Your fingers trail the walls as you walk, running your hands over the images, which feel strange to the touch.

7.1. Vision of the Goddess in the Cave and her presence in the Abyss

The deeper into the passageway you go, the more intricate the magical sigils upon the floor become, and you feel their power as you pass over them. The passageway opens out into a large cave with a bed in the centre. Upon the bed is laid a sleeping woman with a lion at her feet. She is dressed for battle with beautifully tooled leather armour, decorated with silver and gold. Aside her is a sword, a bow with arrows and a spear. She is very tall: her hair is long and red, and very thick. Her facial features look strange, part Chinese, part something else that you cannot quite identify. Around the stone bed are magical symbols that keep her asleep, but the lion has one eye open and is watching you. The lion speaks to you, telling you that you can learn about her by touching her, so you very carefully place a hand upon her leg and close your eyes.

You see her surrounded by humans that look very strange, almost prehuman, and they have ritually brought her into the world as their goddess to lead them in battle and to watch over them. There is something deeper in her, and your sight digs through the layers of magical overlay to find a female deity constructed by angelic patterns and Divine purpose. She is made up of the powers of the elements and directions, and she holds the voice of the forest, of the creatures and of the weather in her. She holds the word of Justice, and keeps the balance not only in nature, but in humanity.

It is then that you realize that she is not fully asleep and that she is watching you using her inner vision. She delves into you, searching your heart and mind as she learns about you. Through that searching, you become aware of imbalances within you that need addressing. She focuses in on aspects of your life that you know you have the power to change. You take your hand off and the contact breaks. Her touch has changed you: your sight is suddenly much stronger and as you cast a glance around the cave, you begin to see that some of the magical sigils that are keeping her in this place are imbalanced and are holding her prisoner against her will and the will of nature. You instinctively spit on to your hand and rub away the sigils on the pathway that block her way out of the Abyss. You can no longer be in this place, and you are told in your mind that you must leave.

Ahead of you is a tunnel that leads away from the direction that you came in, and you are drawn to leave via this tunnel. The minute you step out of the cave you become aware of many strange-looking

7. THE MAGIC OF THE UNDERWORLD

beings who are asleep in the tunnel and you have to pick your way carefully around them. Some look part animal, part human, and others look like nothing you have ever seen before. On the walls of the tunnels are scenes of bloody battles and massacres: you turn your eyes away so that you are not drawn to them as you begin to run down the tunnel. The tunnel has many twists and turns, with entrances to other caves running off of it, but you ignore them and continue to run down the main tunnel. It opens out suddenly onto a large cliff face or what appears to be a massive chasm in the earth. On the other side is a cliff face with similar entrances, and the walls of the cliff sides seem to go down and up forever: this is the great Abyss.

There is a little ledge that you are stood on that juts out slightly into the Abyss so that you can look up and down. As you stand upon the ledge, you remember something deep in your mind about the keeper of the Abyss: the Great Archangel, and you call upon this great being to help you. A pressure builds up in the air around you as a large being emerges out of the depths of the Abyss and looks at you. Explain to this being what you have just done, where you have been and that you wish to go to the Inner Desert so that you can find your way home. As you talk to the angel, you can hear people waking up and someone singing, the noise coming from the tunnel that you have just left. The angel puts out a hand for you to step onto and he lifts you up higher and higher in the Abyss. You see many ledges as you rise, and some of them have strange-looking beings upon them, which look at you as you go past.

The Keeper carefully places you upon the sands of the Inner Desert, and you see that the Sandalphon are already waiting for you. They see the marks upon your forehead, so they know where you have just been and probably what you have just done. One of them places a finger upon your forehead so that you can see into their mind. They show you the greatness of the Goddess that you have just visited, and her importance upon the land, how she keeps it in balance and how she also keeps humanity in balance. You are shown the rituals that bound her and cast her into the Abyss, sending her to sleep in the Underworld, and stopping her process of destruction for balance. Now you understand her better.

The Sandalphon walk with you as you walk towards a mist that will act as a threshold for the Void. They wait as you pass into the mist, passing into the Void and into nothing. You spread out in the nothing, taking in the stillness and silence, being in the place of no time, of no movement. The strain of the long journey you have just taken falls away from you, and you see how important it was for a human to descend into the Underworld, and to pass from the Underworld into the Abyss, and from the Abyss through the Inner Desert and into the Void. It has created a loop, opened a pathway, and reconnected certain powers up. With that knowledge, you step out of the Void and back into the room where you first started. When you are ready you blow out the candle, taking the sacred flame back into yourself, and filling your deep inner landscape with stillness and silence.

★ ★ ★

The loop of travel through the Underworld and Abyss is a very important one and establishes a very necessary pathway that builds regeneration within the land and humanity. Although the above vision is very much about the Goddess, it can be used in many different ways to establish the connection between the ancient past, the present and the future. Such connection is very important for the overall health of humanity and the land, and ensures the passage of ancient knowledge into the distant future. It also enables the freeing up of ancient knowledge that has been bound into the Underworld and allows the beings that accompany such knowledge to emerge out of the Abyss and work with humanity once more. You can see why this work is not really beginner material, as the possibility for abuse is massive and the potential for blowing oneself up with this work is obvious. But is it important work and needs to be expanded upon, developed and worked with a variety of Underworld deities and beings.

7.2 The Sisters at the back of the North Wind

The Sisters are an interesting contact that one finds deep within the earth, with ancient links to the sacred land. (It is not, however, anything to do with the children's book of the same name by George McDonald!)

7. The magic of the Underworld

The Sisters at the back of the North Wind are an ancient line of priestesses who stay as mediators within the land and mediate a destructive power of air out into the world. It is the air within the earth: all elemental forces have a balancing power that flows through them. The air that flows from this contact is the air that changes humanity, the air that carries the disease and change from the depths of the Sea Temple and the air that is part of the weave of fate. They weave the story of the land, the fate of the people and the two opposing land powers, depicted in the UK as the red and white dragons.

For personal work and learning, these sisters will tear you apart in vision and scatter you to the four directions. Then they will reweave you in a fate pattern of magical service. If you work with them in service, you will often find yourself working and weaving land energies or sometimes just weaving or blowing the wind with them. Because they often work with vast stretches of time as far as humanity is concerned, it is often impossible to truly understand what it is you are doing when you work in service with them. Sometimes though, it is possible to see where their work is going and it is a very interesting experience to join in.

The following vision takes you to meet them and be torn apart by them. There is no ritual for working with this contact, as it is not their place to manifest in our time and realm; rather you go to them to work. It is an important step in inner work to touch base with them, if only once, so that you get a deeper understanding of the deeper land powers and how they run through and affect our society.

7.3 Vision of the Sisters at the back of the North Wind

Light a candle and be aware of the candle flame. Close your eyes, and with your inner vision see the candle flame grow bigger and bigger. You are drawn closer to it. The flame suddenly falls through the floor and into the earth, and you are drawn to follow it. You fall through the earth with the flame, falling and falling through rock, tree root, earth and more rock. You fall through caves and tunnels, falling with the flame as it journeys into the Underworld.

7.3. Vision of the Sisters at the back of the North Wind

You find yourself falling in darkness as the surface world vanishes, the way lit only by the flame ahead. You find yourself slowing down and you land in a cave with a high roof and four tunnels, one each in the directions. The flame falls and settles in the centre of the cave and illuminates the space. As you look around, you see that the walls have very old paintings that seem to tell of events from another time. Some of the pictures have graffiti near them, names of people scribbled when they came here and visited. You look closer at the paintings and see stories of the land where you live, of king and queen-ship, and birds and creatures being tended by humans. As you walk around, notice that each tunnel has a carving over the entrance, which itself is carved out of the rock rather than being a natural tunnel. You look closer at each carving and see that they depict the four directions. The entrance to the north has a wind blowing out of it, which makes you curious, and you begin to walk down the tunnel of the north to see what is there.

The tunnel is lit by its own light, a kind of green hue that that glows out from the moss on the walls and allows you to just about see where you are going. A faint voice, singing, reaches you and you listen to it as you walk closer and closer to the source. The tunnel opens out into another cave. This one is smaller, and in the middle of the cave stand three old women with very long hair. They are standing around something you cannot see, and they are singing to it. You draw closer, and one of the old women, without stopping her singing, reaches out and pulls you towards her.

In the centre of the circle of old women is a narrow stone bed, and beneath the bed is a well that falls deep down through the earth and out into the stars. You peer down the well and see the stars faintly in the distance. The old woman holds on to you so that you do not fall in, and begins talking to you. You stand up to look into her eyes as she talks you, even though you cannot understand what she is saying, and her eyes look deeply and sharply into yours. She looks into you, deeper and deeper, seeing the depths of you, seeing your fate, seeing what blocks that fate and seeing where you need to be.

She reaches out a long thin fingernail and scratches you on the forehead, drawing blood. She tastes the blood, looking through your bloodline as she tastes it. When she has seen what she needed to see, she nods and points at the bed: she wants you to get on it. You know

7. THE MAGIC OF THE UNDERWORLD

that if you get on that bed, something powerful will happen and you will never be the same again. So you pause. The old woman rolls her eyes and grabs you, throwing you onto the bed and rolling her sleeves up.

One of the other old women begins to bang something, like metal on stone, creating a beat that the other two women begin to hum and sing to. As they sing, they begin walking around the table, touching you as they turn and singing over you. They dance and sing, turning around as they dance around you, getting a bit faster and a bit faster. Chatter begins in your head and you realize you are hearing conversations you had years ago with various people, some of it from childhood. Then you recognize your grandmother's voice, which then fades into voices you do not recognize. The voices get louder and more jumbled, chanting and calling around you as the women turn and touch you.

Your nose begins to bleed from the pressure, the blood dripping down off of you, off the bed and falling into the stars. Memories of painful emotions in childhood well up in your mind and you begin to cry, your pain and sorrow as a child flooding over you and overwhelming you. Your tears drip off the side of your face and form a small stream of tears that falls with the drops of blood down the well and out into the stars.

The songs of the women become stranger, and sounds begin to combine with the song, the sounds coming from the well of the stars. The song flows up the well, a wordless song of harmonies that is the most beautiful thing you have ever heard. Its pure beauty mixes with the coarse voices of the old women and you are filled with sound of all different pitches and harmonies. The women circle you, weaving your drops of blood with the vibrations of the harmonies falling from the stars. Their circling and calling begins to create a vibration on the rock floor around you, and the vibration slowly gets stronger and stronger. The ground begins to shake and you are forced to hold on to bed for fear of falling off.

The rock bursts open and two beings appear that look like dragons, and yet their flesh seems transparent, as though they were not fully manifest. The two beings rise into the cave, drawn by the call of the old women: these are the two opposing powers of the land.

7.3. Vision of the Sisters at the back of the North Wind

They will appear to you as dragons of two different colours, often red and white, and will wind themselves around each other as they rise into the cave. Immediately the dragons appear the women change the pitch of their song, which now becomes higher and faster. Their weaving becomes more complex and they scoop up the tails of the dragons and begin to weave them into their patterns. You watch in fascination as the women transform the dragons into threads, along with your blood and the vibrations of the stars, and begin making a tapestry. It does not make sense that the sound becomes a thread, nor that the dragons become threads, but you watch as it happens and you stop trying to rationalize it.

Once the tapestry is finished, the women turn to you and begin to circle you while singing. The turning and singing gets faster and faster until you have to shut your eyes so as not to become dizzy. You lie in darkness, feeling a pressure building up around you as the women get faster and the sound gets deeper and stranger. The pressure becomes harder and harder to cope with and you begin to feel like you are going to explode. The air around you presses down upon you and the air in your lungs is sucked out but not replaced. You try and gasp for air, fighting in the confusion of sound and pressure that surrounds you.

The women suddenly change pitch and direction, which creates a massive force that seems to launch you out of yourself. You find yourself out on the land, flowing through trees and rocks, flowing through the air, through animals, passing through buildings, creatures, trees and flowers. You are of no substance, you are pure thought, pure spirit as you pass through all things, experiencing their thoughts and emotions as you pass through them. You are filled with a deep sense of peace and are able to see the beautiful light of Divinity within all things. That light touches you as you pass through things and its touch awakens deep knowledge and deep longing within you. You flow across the land like a breath and the land breathes back in communion. The land calls to you, asking you to become a part of it, to sleep, dream, sing and make love like the earth: to wind your blood into the blood of the land and become one with the sacred earth.

You breathe your reply of love and service of the land, and immediately your ears are filled with the song of the sisters. The song

7. THE MAGIC OF THE UNDERWORLD

seems to take form and you look around you, looking over the face of the land. You see the tapestry that was woven in the depths rise to the surface and settle itself upon the surface of the land. The grass grows through the tapestry that is a weave of your blood, the song of the stars and the dragons of the earth. Trees grow through the tapestry, flowers burst open and birds land upon the earth looking for treats. You flow across the face of the tapestry and recognize the feel of your blood upon its story. That awareness of your blood makes you aware again of your body: your hands reach out to touch the tapestry of the land, and your heart beats with the rhythm of the song.

You are drawn to lie with the tapestry, so you lie down upon the land that holds the story and you feel yourself sink into the tapestry, becoming a part of it. The tapestry wraps itself around you and you feel yourself lay upon and within the land, hearing the heartbeat of the land close to your own. You feel the trees, the rocks, the buildings, the rivers and all the people who live upon the land. They are upon you and you are a part of them. The spirit of the land begins to talk to you, asking you if you would be of service to the land, either in your sleep and dreams, or in your waking life. The land may ask you to sing for it regularly, to garden it, to tend and uphold the land and all the ancestors who sleep within the land. You feel how your life and the land are one, and now you begin to understand the sacrifice of the sovereign king or queen who marries themselves to the land in a act of service. You realize with this work that you must look after your body and act with integrity so that the land stays healthy and balanced.

Once you have decided what you are willing and able to do to be of service to the land, and the land has accepted your proposal, you instantly find yourself back on the table with the three sisters around you. They are turning in the opposite direction, rebuilding you, reweaving your body as they put you back together. You feel the massive change that you have undergone, and you also feel those in the distant past of your bloodline who have done similar unions with the land at one time or another. You feel that deep connection with some of your ancestors, and that connection is woven tight into your memory as the sisters turn around you.

When they have finished, the three women step away from the stone table and wait for you to climb off. You feel unsteady on your

7.3. Vision of the Sisters at the back of the North Wind

feet, your body feels fresh and strong, and your mind feels like it has been opened wide and filled with generations of knowledge regarding the land around you. One of the sisters steps forward to you and marks you upon the forehead: it is the mark of a gardener of the land: one who tends and nurtures the sacred land upon which they live.

The sisters then take you back down through the tunnel to the flame that burns at the centre of the four directions deep underground and they stand you before the flame. You look into the flame and you are drawn to its peace and beauty. You step into the flame, passing through the flame into the Void, the place of eternal stillness and silence. The mark upon your head burns, reminding you of your commitment to serve the land upon which you live. This could mean literal gardening, or simply picking up litter regularly, planting wild flowers, feeding the creatures through the winter, weeding out aggressive plants, tending ancestral graves, or working with the weather when it becomes unbalanced. If you keep up a communion with the land then it will be made very clear to you what needs to happen.

You step out of the Void, through the flame and back into the room where you first started. You pause a while to reflect on what happened before you blow out the candle flame, sending it back into the Void.

★ ★ ★

The Sisters at the Back of the North Wind are an ancient and powerful inner contact group that work with the powers of fate out in the stars and connect/weave them in with the bloodlines of humanity and the deep land powers. Traditionally they are responsible for ancient kingships and queenships, weaving their fate into the land that they will serve so that the land and body become one.

The powers of the land in Britain that they work with often appear to us in myths and legends as streams of red and white that are bound and woven together. Sometimes these streams are depicted as snakes or dragons, and they are the consciousness of the land itself. The contact calls out to the stars, wherein the angelic contacts that work with the stellar fate patterns answer the call in harmonies. The power of the harmonics is mixed with the power of the blood of a sacred female line which in turn is woven into the braid of the red and white dragon powers of the land. This tapestry becomes the fate of the kingship of the sacred land.

The weave of the sisters also manifests the lines of sacred priesthood and other bloodlines that have a direct effect upon the fate of the land and humanity. The blood, stars and the dragon powers combine to create a pattern through which Divinity can manifest through sovereignty, through the fate tapestry that weaves the future of the land and the people. Working with these sisters is very likely to put you into direct contact with these sacred powers, and you may very well find yourself in a long pattern of service to the land where you live. Upon your death you will be expected to sleep within the land or serve the land as an inner contact.

7.4 Origins of humanity in the Abyss

Underworld work, when you strip it right down to its bones, is basically going into the distant past by going down into the layers of the earth. Everything that is no longer reincarnating descends into the Underworld to sleep. That process continues with the consciousness falling ever deeper into the depths, passing into the Abyss and finally vanishing into a compressed layer of consciousness that is eventually recycled. Before it reaches that compression level, anything can be connected with if you are willing to go down deep enough (and you are stupid enough) and the more you interact with something, the nearer it begins to rise back to the surface world. Once something has passed into the Abyss, the connection to the Underworld slowly closes until that ancient consciousness is eventually locked deep in the depths of the Abyss. Those deepest layers cannot generally be accessed by our consciousness as they are just too far removed for us to get to them.

The one thing to really think about before you decide that you want to hack into the depths of ancient humanity is to ask yourself why. If there is a good reason, for example for learning, or for reaching an ancient power that is needed, or to release an ancient deity that was bound etc., then that is fine. But if you are intending

7.4. Origins of humanity in the Abyss

on descending into the very depths of the Abyss for no reason other than sheer curiosity, then you are a moron. The reason you are a moron if you decide to do such a thing, is because the amount of danger that you will encounter on such a mission is akin to bungee jumping off of a 3,000 ft sheer cliff face with a bungee rope that is rather frayed. If you go into any great inner depths without a good reason, then you are basically on your own: other beings will not intervene and waste their energy protecting you just so that you can amuse yourself. But if you are doing a mission in service, for good reason that is not all about you, then a variety of orders of being will intervene and provide you with whatever help you need—but only when you really need it.

When you are reaching back to early forms of humanity, there are a few things you need to think about first. One of those things is the nature of Man itself. For some bizarre reason, modern magicians and spiritual types seem to have a very rosy view about what a human was and how they conducted themselves. There are books-a-many that wax lyrical about our wonderful ancestors living in harmony with nature. Well, yes, true. Except that today's idea of what 'nature' is comes from the Disney channel and has no basis in fact.

Our ancestors did not commune with Bambi, did not talk to the birds in twee 'whistle' talk and did not love the land like their own mother. They were struggling to survive, often against horrific odds, and could not afford to be expressive, cuddly or emotional. Cannibalism was a major feature, for a variety of reasons, as was aggression, selfish use of the land resources and the hostile grabbing of what they wanted when they wanted it. Nothing has changed really. The same is true of the animal world: when you observe animals and birds in a wild environment, you see the same pattern of an aggressive will to survive and reproduce. This only changes when the basics of life are provided, so if you reach back to a time/area when food was in plentiful supply and the population was more or less balanced, then you get very sophisticated and compassionate people in general. But in northern climates or difficult terrain, this was not true.

So bearing that in mind, be aware that some of your most ancient ancestors might very well hang onto you or try to use your body as an energy source or even to climb out of the Abyss. The other thing to remember when you are reaching down deep for a human contact or

7. The Magic of the Underworld

prehuman contact, is that not all human consciousness ends up down the Abyss, it is just one of many areas of universal consciousness where beings go to sleep and dream.

Every place in the Underworld that holds beings has the front door (outer visionary expression) and a back door (the Abyss tunnel). You may find that you have to go down the Abyss, into the tunnel where the ancient ancestor resides, and push through a sealed entrance to emerge out in the Underworld. Bear in mind if you do this, such a door from the Abyss to the Underworld can potentially allow that being access through the Underworld to the surface world. You can bring them into Underworld temples, which usually have lots of checks and balances to keep ancient beings in the Underworld and stop them ascending, and that is usually the safest way to reconnect with an ancient Underworld being that is sleeping in the Abyss. If you have some long-term work with an ancient being, then bringing them into an ancient Underworld temple will be a good working space. Don't try and build your own space in the Underworld as you will not know enough about the ins and outs of the ancient ancestor or being to make it escape-proof. And never, ever, build a tunnel from the Abyss out into the Underworld and up to the surface world: that could potentially wipe out humanity. It would be akin to releasing an ancient form of plague to which we have no immunity.

Working with ancient humans can be very useful in helping us understand our own humanity better, and they can often be brilliant guides/advisors for working with ancient sites, stone circles, etc. They can teach us about star navigation, hunting, weather work, fertility, and power spots upon the land. They can also be very interesting to work with if you are studying the intricacies of genetics from a magical point of view. Just make sure that when the work cycle is over, you help them back to sleep. I assume that you would have the common sense to ask the ancestor in the first place if they would be willing to work with you. Don't just drag them out of sleep: they tend to get a wee bit pissy if you do that. And also be aware that they will have things they want you to do, or things that they need from you. It is always a two-way street.

Some people say that the past and dead should be left in the past, but I do not agree completely with that: the idea of past, present and future is a modern one. If you go back to around 3,000 B.C., you

7.4. Origins of humanity in the Abyss

will find cultures where the dead slept very near or among the living. The communion back and forth between the generations, between the ancients and present day people, was constant. We also talk to the children of the future, keeping an unbroken line of consciousness flowing through and beyond time.

At the deeper levels of the Abyss and the Underworld, you will come across beings that are part human and part reptile-looking. These are not aliens, just a very ancient form of being from this planet. They are very powerful, very magical and are still pretty active in layers of the surface world. They appear still in visions in various parts of the USA where they are still fairly close to the surface. Just tread very carefully with them if you come across these beings: they are very strong and can be very aggressive. These are beings that appeared in Greek myths as Titans, and most places around the world have versions of them.

In any work that you do at great depth in the Underworld, keep tight notes and records of what you do, where you go and what you see: it is still very much exploratory work and generations to come can benefit from your experiences. It can also help you to look back in years to come and start to make connections in your work that were maybe not so obvious at the time.

With Underworld work in general I have found it best, in my own messed-up way, to go down as deep as possible first, do as much exploration as possible, and then slowly ascend, making contact with the various layers of consciousness a layer at a time. I spent a good five years going from the depths, as far back and down as I could go, and then slowly over months and years, exploring more and more layers on the way up. It is fascinating to see the different layers of beings, the layers of temples and sacred places, and then the layers of nonhuman beings who populate the layers a bit closer to the surface. It is also fascinating to work in the Abyss on the opposite side of the Abyss, descending (I always go down slowly in increments when working in the Abyss...I'm a wuss) layer by layer, and contacting the beings in the various layers/tunnels as I go. On the opposite side from us you will find beings who have never expressed themselves in the outer world, who have never had physical manifestation and are not really used to human contact. It can get very interesting.

7. The magic of the Underworld

7.5 Methods of descent

As I said before, when you begin your explorations downwards, first go through the Underworld before you attempt the Abyss at depth. A good practical method of Underworld descent is to go via the various realms so that you are working downwards in stages. First you would go down to the cave of the Goddess, and find a tunnel behind her that leads downwards. Then you would probably find yourself in a cavern where the River of Death flows through, and again there would be a tunnel leading downwards. You will pass through a hall of ancestors, which is basically a large cavern with loads of people sleeping in it (a folktale version is where Arthur's knights are sleeping in a cave in a hill). At this point you have not gone very deep, but you have passed beyond death and are starting to hack through the layers of the past.

Then, again through a tunnel or rough stone stairway, going down you will come to a layer of ancient temples, often with large lioness goddesses in them. These are very good learning places and are also a good place to stop for a breather and allow your physical body to catch up with what you are doing. Pushing further down again you will come to caves that have markings on them, usually very primitive, and holes in the ceiling that seem to reach up to the surface world: these are caves where the roots of certain landmasses and mountain ranges come together and can be worked upon. The magic in these caves is often very powerful, ancient and potentially dangerous. Beyond those caves you will begin to reach volcanic caves, caves with sea water flowing out of them and caves of immense crystal structure.

The beings you will find here are often reptilian and there are many very large complex and powerful beings that can be very difficult to try and communicate with. This is about as far as I got in my explorations. I could say that you cannot go any further, but that would be stupid. It is better to say, I found I could go no further and if I wanted to reach back further I had to cross over into the Abyss. My limitations will possibly not be your limitations.

Once you get as deep as you can go, then you can attempt to cross over into the Abyss from the Underworld. Look very carefully for a blocked up entrance, locked door or very narrow tunnel, etc. If you have got to such depth, it means that others have got here

7.5. Methods of descent

before you, which in turn means that you are at a layer that once held a consciousness that was manifest on the planet surface. If it was manifest, then it has a place in the Abyss, which in turn means that somewhere, there is an entrance to the Abyss from where you are. It may take a while to find it and then a bigger job to actually get it to open. Usually such ancient doorways have guardian demonic beings or angelic beings that are there to stop beings getting out of the Abyss via the Underworld. They are not so bothered about stopping you getting into the Abyss, their attitude being, 'hey dude you want to fry, be my guest.'...

Once you find the entrance, you will need to explain to the guardian, whom you will have just woken up, why you need to access the Abyss. If you reason is good enough, they will open the doorway for you. If you have no service reason, but you are truly and honestly intent upon learning (as opposed to being a tourist) then if you run your hands over the doorway, you will find that certain sigils are carved into the door. If you come across one that has been given to you as a key in the past by an inner contact, you will find it will act as a key to opening the door. The sigil marks you as one in a line of a particular priesthood and as such gives you access to many inner places.

Once through the doorway, you will find yourself in a tunnel that will eventually lead to a large cavern or series of caverns. This is the 'real' abode of the beings from the Underworld realm whose level you are at. Beyond that series of caverns will be another tunnel which will lead to the Abyss itself, and it will have a ledge that overhangs the Abyss slightly. Standing on that, you will be able to call the Keeper of the Abyss who will lift you up to the Inner Desert which is the layer in the Abyss in which we humans currently reside. If however you wish to explore the Abyss a bit more, you will find a stone stair carved out of the rock face of the Abyss which basically goes all the way up while visiting many of the ledges on the way. Each ledge is marked with magical patterns and veils which stop beings that are down the Abyss, and belong there, from using the stairway to rise up. You will have to be very careful if you use this stairway to explore or access some of the tunnels: make sure that you do not have any hitchhikers attached who will use you to get out. On our side of the Abyss, which is also the side that the Underworld opens out onto, reside all beings

7. THE MAGIC OF THE UNDERWORLD

or parts of the consciousness of those beings that have at one time or other manifested in the outside world, i.e. our universe. The caves and tunnels on the opposite side of the Abyss are the resting places of the beings which have never physically manifested at all. So for example, from the Inner Desert, which is our layer, on the opposite side of the Abyss, going down to the first layer of caves and tunnels is the faery realm.

The basic rule of thumb, when exploring the Abyss from down to up, is to use your common sense. Trust nothing, dress as anything but human, and keep on your side of the Abyss. Do not be tempted to cross over and explore down the other side: the Abyss can only be safely crossed from our own layer of the Inner Desert, unless you are working with angelic beings. If you do it may be very possible that you will not come back. Working 'down' at depth has been sadly neglected for thousands of years and it is time for reconnection, service and communion once more.

From a body maintenance perspective, be aware that going deep down into the Underworld and Abyss is akin to deep sea diving. It will affect your body in a variety of ways and you will without doubt have a physical impact from the work. Ensure when you are undertaking a program of deep Underworld work that you have regular body care treatments like acupuncture or cranial osteopathy: you will basically need putting back together again afterwards. Ensure that you are taking vitamins or are on a really healthy diet, and get loads of sleep between work sessions. The body heals when it sleeps, and also the work will continue in a way that your body can adjust around.

Working deeply in the Underworld has a side effect of grounding you, connecting you with your ancestors and their skill sets, and giving you good solid roots to work from. As a magician, it is the most important part of your development and will help you to really come to know yourself, which is the greatest achievement that any of us can truly reach.

Chapter Eight

Functioning as an adept

What does it mean to be an adept? In truth, and in my world, it is not a title assigned to a member of an order upon completion of training and tests, but a description of someone who has done a lot of training, maturing and self-development, someone with real skills, knowledge and technique, and someone who has matured beyond the self and is ready for service/work at a deeper level. This takes decades of work, and to get to a full working adept power level takes at least into your forties or fifties if you began as a teenager. I find it hilarious that there are twenty-somethings who have done a couple of years of postal study, attended a few weekend workshops in a 'Mystery school,' and declare themselves to be adepts: my question would be, adept at what precisely?

To be an adept means to be a person who has in-depth knowledge of a wide variety of advanced magical skills, and who can practically apply those skills with consistency, maturity and honour. Most importantly, *they know what it is that they do not know.*

We never arrive at a completion of the adept stage: in magic the learning is lifelong and just when you think you 'know,' another layer of the magic emerges, and the learning starts all over again. That is if the magician has developed a learning method: when you are 'taught' something by a teacher, you do not really develop an independent learning method, which with magic in particular means the magician can develop a lifelong dependency on teachers. In such cases the magician never really reaches adepthood: they become eternal initiate students.

The development of the independent learning method comes from downright curiousness: the need to know what is under ever stone, the need to learn as much as possible without a teacher, and the ability to pay proper attention to the smallest details, while

8. Functioning as an Adept

also taking responsibility for everything that you do. Being able to continue to the bitter end of a learning curve without giving in or stepping back in the face of adversity or threat. All of these qualities and more create not only a strong potential adept, they also by nature of walking a magical path that way, create a learning method that is often unique to the individual. In the ancient world, and really until the last hundred years or so, an initiate was trained by being given one step and they were expected to find the other ninety-nine steps for themselves: that is true magical learning.

The achievement of the skill level (rather than title) of adept also brings with it certain responsibilities. If a person is very self-obsessed, then the concept of true magical service will be alien to them and it is pretty certain that they will not reach the depth of power needed to be a true adept. It is very rare for a totally selfish person to move beyond initiate level simply because the skill level of adept involves a lot of selfless work. Why? Because a large amount of an adept's ability to do heavy lifting in magic comes from cooperation with other beings and powers. If you do not help others when needed, then inner/spirit beings will not work with you: it is always a two-way street. First you give freely and without agenda, so that you are recognized as one who works as part of the larger universal pattern in an active magical way. Once recognized as such, your own work and fate becomes an active part of that pattern and when the need arises, other magicians in other times, along with inner contacts, spirits, deities and beings will step forward and help you when you need it.

8.1 Service

Your magical skills may be called into the service of any religion be it present or past, or even future: though the call usually only comes if magic has been used in that religion and it has all slowly gone horribly wrong. If the degeneration in a religion is natural, then it is not a situation for magicians to interfere with. It is irrelevant what you think of the religious structure: your job is to ensure that it is plugged in and the lights are on. If the religion has degenerated beyond all saving, then it is the adept's job to pull the plug out and leave them in the dark. You cannot make this vast decision yourself: the job will come to you through inner contacts or sometimes even from the deity of the religion itself.

This might all read as a very controversial and interfering way of working, but in truth, if done unconditionally, and the degeneration came from magic in the first place, then it is simply magical service. If a religion has become so degenerate that humanity cannot reach Divinity through it and everything has been tried to plug it back in and failed, then the structure has no function in the future: it must be dismantled to ensure that parasitical elements do not move in and begin to operate it, though usually in such situations the vessel of the religion is likely to be heavily parasited already. It is basically the responsibility of the priesthood to close down a spiritual structure to prevent that from happening. If the priesthood has degenerated enough to have lost that skill, then it falls to whoever has the ability, usually the magicians.

In earlier times, when the priest/esshood knew that the end was coming, be it war, famine, or just the end of the shelf life, they would close the gates that allowed Divinity to step into the deity, and basically shut off the link between the Inner Temple and the outer. This can be directly experienced at some ancient temple sites where you can go to an altar area, or an inner sanctum and try to commune with the deity there. Not only will you not get anything, the silence will be deafening. It is emptier that an empty space: it is as if the very life has been sucked out of a space: that is how a lockdown is experienced. They can be unlocked, but you must be ready to take responsibility for whatever happens if you do open it all back up. You would probably have to move the whole structure to where you could work regularly with it.

If you are called to do such work and you are not sure of the ethics of such an action, (and such questioning of one's ethics and motives it very important) then go into the Inner Temple structure of the religion. Often the inner structures still exist and have priesthoods working within them. Talk with them and see what they suggest. Often, when a religion has degenerated for long enough, the inner priesthoods cut the outer structure loose. The one thing you have to really remember is you cannot be judge and jury for a religious structure: it has to be a call from the Inner Worlds. Even if a religion has degenerated to a point where it is killing and torturing

8. Functioning as an Adept

people, so long as Divinity is flowing through the structure, it is not your concern: destruction is just as important as creation and stasis. Everything, both good and bad, has an action in building the future, and you always, as an adept, have to be for neither good nor bad, for neither right nor left hand path: your job is simply to work. Humans do not have a long enough lifespan to understand the very long-term patterns of how things evolve: bad can bring great good, good can trigger great evil, so you must work without emotion, without judgement, doing only what is requested to bring things to where they need to be.

Usually such a call comes from the inner only when magic was used originally in the religion for conditional purposes and where the degeneration over time is a direct result of that conditional magic. Natural decay is usually left alone, and that has always been my policy too. If magic caused the problem, then use magic to mop it up, if it is a natural process, then let it be. Most if not all of my work as an exorcist over the years was a matter of cleaning up magical messes and putting away beings that had been brought into our world by magic. When I was called out to a situation that was natural, I just used to use common sense, compassion and priesthood skills to open the gates to let confused and trapped souls out.

That is just one example of one area of work that an adept can sometimes be called to. Basically the types of work that present can be limitless, so it is pointless trying to create 'work boxes' of what adepts 'do.' It is much less a matter of 'what,' and more of 'why.' The more experienced as an adept you become, the less magical work you actually do. But when you do take action, it is powerful, to the point, and very much needed. Just bear in mind that if you choose to go down the road of conditional magic, the complex strands of fate connections and the energetic deficits they create can eventually balloon out of control and you could spend the rest of your life trying to undo, rebalance etc. It's all about choices.

One area of very interesting work that an adept can get drawn into is joining in very long-term work. You step in and take up where others have left off, do the best that you can for as long as you can, and then you hand off to the next person coming up. Usually these long-term jobs are to do with the land, civilization, and the survival of humanity. Sometimes it is maintaining places like the Abyss, or working in the death realm, working on the weaving of the fate of nations, or helping clean up land messes that will take generations (like nuclear dumping). Again the list is endless, but the jobs are big, hard work and you get no recognition whatsoever. What you do get is immense learning, very good skill practice and the knowledge that your grand-kids' offspring will probably have a better, more fruitful life because of your work. You can also assign yourself to a term of service with a specific priest/esshood and help to maintain and clean up lineages, temples, and magical patterns.

The most curious form of adept service is to just be yourself. You do no inner magic, just the occasional prayer if anything: you just live your life and affect unconditional change just by being where you are and doing ordinary things while magic flows freely and naturally through you and out into the world. Once you have done a great deal of inner magical work over a long period of time, you can effect change just by turning up and being at a place or around a person. At that stage of adeptship, you cannot turn the magic on and off: it is constantly flowing through you all the time. You become the open gate between the outer and Inner Worlds, and you will find yourself being sent to places or people just to be there. You will go away wondering what the hell that was all about, but you will find that your visit coincided with a major change: you were the energetic catalyst that was needed. People will find their way to you, will be drawn to you, and you will bring change to their lives just by being around them.

You can immediately see how this can very easily send a magician on a massive ego trip. You have to be very careful to understand that it is not such a major thing to be an energetic catalyst: in fact, it is quite a small role indeed. You are nothing but a doorway, a postman, a servant. You are not the messiah and you cannot wield that power to suit your own ego or yourself: it simply will not work, as it ultimately does not, as a power, originate from within you, you are a mere stepping stone. The other truth to bear in mind is that you are not special, just trained. If you fell over tomorrow, there would be someone right behind you to take up your path: always remember that you are and always will be truly expendable and replaceable.

Once you step onto the path of true magical adeptship, regardless of what that path is, be it destruction, regeneration or maintaining something, you will find the Sword of Justice dangling precariously over your head. With great power comes a heavy price, and that price is honour and responsibility. Just as in the story of Damocles, where the king appears to have limitless wealth, power and riches, so he also has the sword of Justice hanging by a thread over his head. In the story, the king dangles the sword by a hair to demonstrate to Damocles just how dangerous it can be. But that story is a fragment of one of the secrets of the Mysteries: the more power you gain, the more accountable you become. For an adept, that translates, in really simple terms, to doing nothing you know to be wrong or selfish, as you will get an instant karma rebalance, which is often very unpleasant.

8.2 Practicalities of living as an adept

I have broached some of these issues in the other books, but there are certain points I want to reiterate here in more depth as they are important. The deeper in magic you go, the more it affects your body and your life: this is just one of those truths that there is no escaping, no matter how much you want to deny it. The type of magic that you do will define the type of reaction your body will have, and the reaction will be specific to your own body. It will open out weaknesses and aggravate certain conditions, and if you are working in an unbalanced way, it will trigger certain illnesses.

Because of the high level of power that is flung around when an adept is working, it really helps you to survive those levels of power if you look after your life and body in a way that cushions the blows. There are no hard and fast rules, so this is more like a heads-up to be more attentive to your body, your family and your surroundings. If you are eating something that your body cannot process properly or is intolerant of, then the reaction will be far greater than it would be if you were not doing magic. If you do magic when you are ill, say with a cold, then it will potentially develop into a more serious viral condition. Some people would look upon this as a bad thing and say that magic is bad for the body. In fact, the reverse is true. What is happening is that your body is no longer tolerating your stupidity and is forcing you to behave yourself.

8.2. Practicalities of living as an adept

The power of the magic will change things in your life that need changing: it will sweep away old and no longer relevant aspects of your life. That really starts to happen in the initiate phase and is usually settling by the time you get to be a trained and working adept. The idea of the initiate phase, from an inner perspective, is to clean you up and clean up your life. By the time you are an adept it is about putting you to work and smacking your wrist if you do something silly.

So as an adept, you will begin to find that everything that comes in and out of your life has a major purpose, and that you are put into places or situations where either you have a job to do, or your presence is needed as a catalyst. Life becomes one major job. There is no time out, and it is not something you can walk away from at this stage: you become inexorably linked to the karma of the land, civilization and the deities. You will be pulled into service whenever you are needed, and your life will flow with the rhythm of the land. Everything and anything around you will have meaning and power, and you will have to be very careful about what you are talking to: every statue or cuddly toy that you choose to chat to could potentially become a window for a being to step into.

You can see how important it is when walking such a path to have a strong dose of common sense and to keep the ego under control. It is hard enough for a very stable person to operate under these conditions, so imagine what it is like for someone who has a mental fragility or a tendency towards mental illness: magical work at this level would push them way over the edge and far away.

It is very important to really get a sense for what is real and what is imagined, for very obvious reasons, and it is also very important to constantly question your ability, your motives and your actions. If you can walk that thin line, you will find yourself in a world where everything is magical, everything has Divine Presence, and everything truly talks to you. Every action you take has long-term consequences, so you learn to be thoughtful with your actions and to be constantly listening to the land which provides all the guidance you need. I once mentioned this to a magician friend of mine who retorted that he did not do 'nature' magic and therefore would not commune with the land. What a stupid thing to say: the land is all around you, it is what upholds you, feeds you, and gives you shelter.

It is not a fashion accessory like a pentacle that you choose to wear or not; it is a vast power expression of Divinity all around you. Whether you are into nature magic or not, the land processes power. It is the altar of the greatest temple of all.

8.3 Working within a tradition

If you are working as an adept within a specific magical tradition (i.e. as a real adept, not a purchased or dressed-up one) then the field range of your work will be fairly narrow and intense. In contacted lodges and specific lineages of magic, the adepts are responsible for keeping the line of magic clear and balanced. They also interact intensely with the inner contacts to clear away anything that is disrupting or degenerating the magical line. The adept will often work in the past, clearing out energetic tangles of magic from generations before, and working with the deities to help weave magical patterns for the future. Those patterns will be the template for the lodge in the future to ensure its healthy survival. It will also ensure that the lodge or group has a healthy foundation that allows its initiates to get on with its long-term project work, while the adepts working with the initiates on those projects will tap into the patterns to continually stabilize them.

Often, the work of a lodge that is operating at this level tends to be work that is long-term service to a landmass, a deity or a monarchy. The adepts not only work with the initiates in these long-term projects, they enable the projects to happen by keeping the doors open, bridging the deity and being the catalyst. The difference between an adept working in a lodge and an adept working 'freelance' for want of a better word, is that the 'freelance' adept will have a much greater responsibility, a wider field of service, and will not be limited by a belief system or an agenda. Personally, I feel that freelance is the better way to work: you answer to no one other than yourself and the Gods.

8.4 The future: passing on the teaching

It is important to pass the work on from generation to generation, to keep the flame going. This can be done through writing, group teaching or one-on-one apprentices. A major word of warning: this is the last true test and step for an adept: can you pass on the work without making yourself terribly important, a messiah or a guru? When you teach, and you teach things that are worth teaching, then people listen. When people listen to what you are saying, you realize what potential 'power' you have over people, and it is a temptation to bask in the fact that people look up to you. Yes, people will idolize you, yes, they will write to you asking you to be their teacher, and yes, people will put you high up there on a pedestal. It's a long way to fall, and it can be a painful fall.

When you take on the role of teacher you also take on the responsibility for the development of other people. That is a major responsibility in itself, not only because you are the one who will put them on their magical path, but also because you are the one who has to burst all of their bubbles, glue their feet to the ground, and slap them around the back of the head when they make mistakes. You cannot do that to others until you can first do it to yourself.

A magical training is also soul training, a development of the personality and a maturing of the consciousness. As a teacher you are responsible for putting the student in the path of experiences that will potentially trigger that development, for taking them to places that they need to learn about, and for introducing them to working methods that will help them learn to learn properly. It truly is a massive responsibility: you are the doorway that allows Divinity and Humanity to experience each other: keep that in mind.

Unfortunately these days, many magicians/occultists have taken up the fashion pedestal of the workshop guru. These magicians teach general magical workshops that are cloaked in publicity hype about being 'secret teachings,' 'never before seen Mysteries' or 'advanced archaic magical techniques' which are actually all just ordinary magic, or even made up stuff that sounds good but has no real content. They are expensive, exclusive and just plain useless as a form of magical training. They may offer certain experiences that are of interest, but

8. Functioning as an Adept

at the end of the day, they are like candy bars: tasty, fun, filling for a short while, but with no real nutritional value whatsoever.

Some books have become like that also, and it truly is a minefield for the aspirant to find a teacher whose source of information is reliable, understandable and walks the real path. There is a lot of dross that one has to plough through, but that in itself can be a good part of the training: learning discernment the hard way can be a valuable lesson indeed. Discernment is a skill that is invaluable on a magical path of learning. There is also a lot of good writing and teaching out there, usually happening quietly and without major fanfares. If the student has true intent to walk and develop upon a magical path, they will stumble across books, teachers, mentors and friends as and when they need to: that is how it works. One of the jobs of an adept is to be there for a student to stumble across: guide them for as long as they need it, and *then let them go when they need to move on.* Never try to hold on to a student. An adept teacher is always a stepping stone, nothing more.

There is a lot of responsibility upon your shoulders if you choose to be of service by teaching, and yet it is a very rewarding path to walk down. The basic rules for avoiding the ego pitfalls while being a good teacher are:

Don't involve money. If you have to travel a distance or hire a venue, then expenses are fine: it shouldn't cost you anything to teach. But charge no fees—and don't try to circumvent that rule to get money while kidding yourself you are still doing service. Money can quickly destroy a good teacher: I have seen it happen often. How? Once you teach for money, you become dependant upon the income and you gradually begin tailoring the work to ensure enough people turn up to make the amount of money that you need. Often the magic that truly needs teaching is work that will not be popular at all, and therefore will not make much money as it will not draw a large or consistent crowd. You can see how this can unfold into a situation where the Mysteries are rewritten to be more palatable, more commercial, and more like product, or the teacher starts to teach the latest magical fashion fad, working with the latest fashionable deity and with the latest fashionable tools. This is not a new story, but it is a story that has destroyed many a good magician who tried to make a regular income from peddling popular teaching in courses and workshops. Kidding yourself and others that you can work for money without falling into that trap is just fooling yourself, and it will bring about the eventual destruction of your work. The door will slam shut to the inner contacts—they will simply withdraw from you, and you will be left as a parody of what you could have been.

Always remember you are not special. You are not saving the world, you are not forming a religion, and you are not the only holder of the information.

Make the information you are teaching accessible, simple and straight forward. There is no need to dress magical work: it dresses itself. I am sick to death of seeing books of magic that are so wordy, complex and obscure as to be incomprehensible, and yet they are usually pretty empty of anything magical or meaningful. There is no point or purpose to doing that other than masking the fact that you have not got a clue about the subject matter you are writing on.

Never ever hold back information, teachings or patterns to make yourself more knowledgeable than your students. This is a major trap some magical teachers get into. Your students should surpass you, not lag behind you. The information is not yours to hold back: you are just a messenger boy and the magical knowledge should flow through you unhindered at all times. If you play power games with the information and the students, then the inner connections will fade off and the contacts will walk away from you, only to be replaced by parasites set on amusing themselves at your expense.

Never get into sexual power games with your students and coworkers. This is another favourite with the guru types. Sex in this day and age is something between two people who love each other, or who just want sex, and it is not part of magical work, no matter how much you try to bullshit yourself. If you use sex with your students to gratify yourself, to gain power or to play power games, then you are degenerate and will fall to the bottom of the heap magically.

Many if not all of the above are traps that many adepts have fallen into and various lodges have grappled with them in one way or another. Just do not go down that road: grow up and get real about yourself: know yourself and your limitations. And then go out into the world and be useful.

8. Functioning as an Adept

wsḫ jst nt hr m mdww
spd dsw r th mjtn

Broad is the place of one calm in speech,
Sharp the knives against one who oversteps the Path.

— *The Instruction of Kagemni's Father*

Appendix A

Advanced Decoys

*an extract from Quareia the Adept: Module V (Advanced Magic, Lesson 7)
by Josephine McCarthy*

A magical decoy is essentially a vessel with a close resonance to some target or victim. It draws the incoming magic to itself due to its resonance with the target. It takes in the magic, absorbs it, and holds it. If the incoming power or magic is ongoing rather than a one-off, then the decoy will continue to absorb the magic until it can hold no more power, at which point it will self-destruct. Some decoys can keep going success- fully for a long time; others cannot. It depends on what it is, what it is made of, and so forth.

Decoys can absorb natural flows of power, like death waves, destruction tides, and so forth; and they can also absorb directed magical attacks. Once the decoy is working, it will continue to work in the background and the magician can forget about it and get on with their work.

If the magician has to travel and they are on the receiving end of a prolonged attack, or their personal pattern is somehow attracting a prolonged destructive pulse, then often inner contacts will deposit a temporary decoy in their path. If you are paying attention and spot the temporary decoy, and engage it, then it will step into action and provide you with protection until you get back home.

Sometimes decoys can work for beginners. An adept can teach a beginner about them as a magical 'trick' if they are in direct danger— rare, though it does happen. But quite a few decoys work due to the adept's past work, resonance, and contact. This is why this lesson has to be in the adept section, as it does not work the same for someone not contacted or an apprentice. It is a seemingly simple method of

A. Advanced Decoys

magic, but its simplicity belies the fact that a lot is going on behind the scenes.

If you have to put together a decoy for a beginner or non-magical person, always use divination to ensure that it will actually work, and that you have chosen the right decoy. Choosing right can be a skill in itself, as you have to think poetically as well as magically.

Just remember that decoys are just *decoys*. They do not deflect, they do not defend, and they work due to their simplicity. They do one job, to divert, and nothing more.

Let's look at a few examples of decoys, how they work, and why.

A.1 Personal decoys

The most obvious and most-used decoy is an image, or doll, of the person. We have looked at this a little before. The method can also be applied in reverse, as it is in some folk magic involving *poppets*, where the poppet is attacked to affect the person.

Any such magic is a two-way street, and the more formed the decoy, the more chance there is that it can be used in reverse. Because of this, adept magicians rarely use personal decoys, as so much can go wrong with them. But if one can be carefully looked after in the long-term then it can work to provide a layer of protection—as well as other things— from heavy, prolonged, incoming fire.

The doll is placed near where the magician sleeps, and is made to look as much as possible like the magician, including any tattoos, etc. Once its job is done, it should be placed carefully in a box where it will not be disturbed and put in long-term storage. Once an energetic connection is made between the doll and the magician, it is very hard to break without physically or energetically damaging the magician. This is why this method is not often deployed. There are ways of disconnecting the link that are used in West African and Caribbean magic, but I do not know enough about them, nor have I successfully worked those methods enough myself, to write about them.

When you deploy a personal decoy, you rarely have to do much magic at all: they trigger automatically as a result of your magical work, the contact already within and around you, and the incoming threat. It is more of a coming-together of energetic elements at the right time; and if you begin to treat the doll as a personal decoy then it will start to take on that role.

Another form of personal decoy is having someone with the same name, physical features, or identical fate spots: a doppelgänger. This is not something you can magically produce or manipulate, but sometimes inner contacts will put a doppelgänger near you when you are in real danger and it is important that you survive. Again, this happens as a result of your work as an adept and is one of the things done for you to maintain your magical service—what you give, you also receive.

The main reason for mentioning this type of decoy is that when you spot it—and it does become obvious—you know that a real danger is flowing towards you. That lets you deploy other layers of protection in different ways, so that you can create a weave of very different types of deflection and protection, as well as having the doppelgänger. Protective layers used like this are much harder for a hostile magician to hack through, whereas a single protection can be dispensed with much more easily.

If the victim of an attack has a common name, and citizenship of more than one country, that will already create a dilemma for an attacker. The majority of magicians who would undertake such an attack use a name, an image or photograph, and a personal detail—that is if they do not have some personal belonging of yours. Many magicians assume that the being who deliverers the attack goes by the details it is given, but this is a mistake: those details are translated into fate points and patterns, and the being sees those, not the victim's face, name, and hair.

If you are near people with similar or identical sets of fate spots, the being has choices. If its job is to destroy, then it will look for the weakest, easiest option.

Say, for example, that a being was sent to attack me, and the attacker used my name and image to direct it. It would seek out a grey-haired woman called Josephine McCarthy who is involved in magic *and who stubbed her toe against the wall four days ago.* And that last detail is the important one that many magicians would forget about. Fate power points, i.e. hotspots that are potential junctions in

A. Advanced Decoys

a fate pattern and are therefore 'shinier' or more visible can often be seemingly tiny, unimportant events.

Thousands of women in Ireland share my name, have grey hair, and are involved in some way with magic—often folk magic dressed up as local tradition. And at least one of them will have banged her foot within four days of me banging mine. If one of them is very elderly, and therefore weak, then the attack will 'out' itself through that unfortunate person.

Bear in mind that a lot of your protection as an adept does not come from magical protection you have put in place, but from the beings and contacts around you and the magical patterns you have built over the years. You may not be even aware of an incoming attack: it will be deflected, decoyed, and moved around you so that you can get on with your work. You may feel a small part of it in the form of a drop in energy, the sudden appearance and attentiveness of beings around you, or in your dreams; but you will likely not pick up on what is actually happening until elderly people with similar patterns to yours start dropping around you.

I see this as more of a magical curiosity than anything to do with magical technique; but as an adept, being aware of this phenomenon and its implications for you can serve as an advance warning that you need to be careful, and that it may be time to go undercover for a little while. This dynamic has little or no effect in less experienced magicians, but the Fates weave and deflect as necessary when an adept is doing service work or has a very fateful future.

A.2 False doors

False doors are another decoy. They are used in tombs, temples, and magical work spaces. These are not about averting a personal attack or destructive pulse, but are more about protecting a space from magical intrusion or from being gate-crashed by beings.

For the most part the work done in the magical space and its continuous tuning will create a barrier that stops anything accessing the space. However, if a long-term pattern is to be triggered in a workspace and the magicians will be withdrawing for a lengthy period of time to let the inner powers get on with the work without the

A.2. False doors

magicians re-entering, then sometimes a decoy door is needed to stop intruders.

Sometimes—rarely—the following type of magical work is conducted - a place is tuned, empowered, and a series of visionary rituals are done to trigger a pattern into formation. Then, instead of the pattern being released, it is held in the space for a prolonged period of time. The room is never entered, and the inner beings and powers in the pattern work alone, without further human intervention. This is done when the pattern is upkeeping something powerful out in the world, and if the pattern is disturbed it could fall apart.

In such instances, besides the usual guardians and deflections, door decoys are deployed to confuse and repel inner beings and invasive magicians working in vision. Sometimes an altar is placed before the door with food offerings to keeping an intruding spirit busy.

Such false doors were used in Ancient Egypt from the third dynasty in mortuary temples and the sacred temples themselves. They, too, would sometimes have altars for food offerings before them. Archaeologists think that these false doors acted as thresholds for the deities and spirits of the dead. This is likely correct for the most part, in which case they were not working as decoys, but as thresholds. Personally though, when I have come across some false doors in temples and mortuary temples that have often led in vision to energetic 'mazes.'

So do not assume that every false door you see is a decoy, or that they are all thresholds. Sometimes they are one or the other; sometimes they may even be both. In many Egyptian temples the false door is on the west wall of a remote chapel, or at the back of the temple. So again, there may be a different function for those. I suspect that this is one of those situations where one thing can have different applications. If you come across one in a building, the best way to find out what it does is to try and use it to access a space in vision and see what happens.

In inner magical temple construction false doors are deployed as decoys, and often have very intricate carvings or reliefs around them with lots of words or patterns to keep a curious spirit busy—and

A. Advanced Decoys

a gate-crashing magician confused. If an inner place really needs protecting then false doors can be constructed that lead to mazes, 'false chapels,' or fake work spaces. They are constructed using inner vision and patterning, and are used to filter out the curious and uninitiated.

If you are lucky enough to have a proper, dedicated magical space then it can be a very interesting and useful experiment to paint a false door near or next to the real one on the outside the magical space, and see what a difference it makes. I once lived in a house that had two front doors, one of which was false, and it did make a difference to the flow of beings in and out of the house.

A.3 Time decoys

This is a curious one that I learned purely by accident. It was one of those situations where necessity brings forth a solution. When I sat back and analysed what was going on from a magical perspective, I discovered that fate patterns and inner 'drivers' of events were *particularly sensitive to time.*

Before we get to the actual decoy, let me explain a little of what I went on to discover about time and magic. With a natural wave of destruction or death, or a magical attack, part of what makes that power successfully reach its target is time. Our fate patterns are huge and complex, and the various different magical and mundane elements, *including time,* that make up a fate hotspot have to be in perfect alignment for the power to properly out itself as a fully manifested event. If time is confused, then the person is either sideswiped rather than getting the full hit, or they avoid the hit altogether.

I found this very curious and I realized that at certain times of magical danger I was not getting the full-on hit that was aimed at me. One thing those times had in common was that 'time,' or more precisely, *the measurement of time* around me was out of sync. I started to experiment, and I became fascinated.

I have a problem with watches and digital clocks. They quickly start go out of sync around me and watches invariably die within a week or two of my wearing them. The more technologically advanced the timepiece, the quicker it runs down and stops. As I grew older, clockwork timepieces in the house were slowly replaced by battery-operated or electric ones, and they all began to keep different times. I have always tended to have a lot of clocks around me, as I had a weird obsession with keeping the right time—which is a bit unfortunate if you affect timepieces!

I found that if I stopped continually resetting clocks to the right time, and just let them do their own thing, then not only did it slowly wean me from my time obsession, but I also noticed that the heavy tides and occasional attack aimed at me dissipated in the house. Interesting. I wondered if it was just a coincidence, and the deity powers around me were doing more than providing their usual layer of help and protection.

Later, I had to live in a house with no magical tools, deities, objects, or anything. I was having downtime away from magic to protect my children from an acrimonious divorce that included hostile magical aspects. The only weird thing in the house was how its five clocks all kept different times. Some were an hour out, some were twenty minutes or so out, and one of them repeatedly stopped. I also found that heavy incoming fire was being dissipated in the house, even though it was magically shut down.

After a marathon divination session to try and pinpoint what exactly was working and what was not, I managed to identify the time confusion in the house as a layer of energy that was giving me protection. This did not make sense to me at first, as time, in my mind, was just *there*, and the clocks were simply measuring it. However, it appeared that my observation of time, and my use of time as a tool in my everyday life made it an integral part of my mundane pattern. I always look at clocks, and through observing my use of time, I realized that I focused on the time that was specific to the room I was working in. If I went into another room that had a different clock with a different time, I immediately refocused into that 'time frame': essentially my consciousness was 'time jumping' in terms of how it organized itself. Or to put it another way, each room was its own universe.

I began to experiment. I took out most of the clocks and kept only a very accurate one. The energy of magical attacks came in like

A. Advanced Decoys

a tsunami. I put the clocks back, set them to slightly different times, and let them go out of time as they tended to do around me. Bingo: the energy thrown at me dissipated considerably. It did not get rid of it totally, but it took out a lot of its sting. I got a very mild sideswipe instead of the full-on attack.

I took it a bit further. I got a day-to-day calendar and put it up, but I always left it a couple of days out of date. I let the clocks meander about in their own little time world, and I also changed my front door number to something wrong. Then I had my first truly peaceful night's sleep in months. Was this purely psychological? I was not sure.

The next time I was contacted by a magician under attack, one that used the same type of magic aimed at me, I suggested they get three or four clocks, keep one in each living space, and set them all to different times. I told him to take off his watch and simply go by the clocks in his house. Within twenty-four hours the power of the attack had lessened considerably. He contacted me very excitedly to tell me it had worked, but some was still getting through. I then told him about the calendar and the door number. Within three days of him trying them, life was back to normal.

The attack was still going on, but it was fragmenting when it got to the confused exterior presentation of time and place in the house. What bits did get through, the target's guardians mopped up.

Remember about working in layers? This is a far better method than constantly doing protective rituals or workings, or having large stomping guardians circling your house, or constantly having to do talismans. It is simple, effective, and you can leave it to work while you get on with your life.

However, sadly, when I tried this technique on a non-magical person in the path of destruction, it did not work. I tried it a few times more with non-magical people or magical beginners, and it still did not work. Yet it worked for all the more advanced magicians I told about it. Once more I was curious: why? I was pushed back on observation and divination.

The time decoy, like some other decoys, works due to the magician's magical patterns and tuning. I discovered that when you work magic at an adept level, your fate pattern becomes highly tuned and focused, and that little things can be deployed as a distraction from that highly tuned pattern. Time for an adept is a major element of their pattern, and it can become very defined, right down to the minutes.

This does not mean you are locked into a restrictive fate pattern; quite the opposite, in fact. It means that the more power and contact you work with as an adept, the more sensitive your pattern becomes to the slightest variation in key elements like time, place, and so forth. It is like the lens becomes highly tuned.

This sensitivity of timing plays itself out through an adept's the everyday life. They will be delayed by something so that they arrive at exactly the right moment; they will choose a seemingly random date which will turn out to be highly significant or perfect timing; or clocks will start to fail around them if they need to be in a confused time.

Funnily enough, the village where I live has an ancient church and bell tower with a clock. It was always known to keep great time, and the locals used to set their clocks by it. Then I moved in. Now it is rarely right and sometimes goes out by hours. As well as my house of clocks that all live in their own time universes, any power sensitive to time will not get anywhere near me.

A.4 Oppositions

Oppositions are a poetic way of triggering a decoy that also balances something. Again it draws on what is in the magician in terms of skill, contact, and patterns; and it can be used when an energetically affecting presence has been brought into being by another magician.

For example—and this is a real example—a certain group of magicians are social friends but do not work together at all. They get together occasionally throughout the year at conferences, and so forth. Though they do not and never have worked together, being in the same social circle still creates a pattern, as they are all working in magic, albeit different forms.

Once, one of those magicians jokingly got a toy creature and started talking to it. He treated it like a person and projected onto it all the 'naughty' things he could not do in life. He started to create

A. Advanced Decoys

narratives about the creature, how it was a demon who got up to all sorts of dubious activities. That narrative began to expand to include the creature having an active sex life: it was treated as a person.

Over time the toy became a vessel for a hungry and very intelligent parasite which fed off the magician. The magician was politely warned of what was happening, but he chose to ignore the warning. The toy became a strong vessel, which gave the parasite a stronger presence in the physical world. Then the parasite started to reach out to the other magicians in the social circle to try and connect with them, and a very unhealthy situation slowly developed.

The magician had not projected something of himself into the toy at all; rather he had created the vessel by talking to the toy and treating it as a living being. When you do that the intent, character, and purpose you have in your uttering tends to define what sort of vessel it becomes, which defines what sort of being would want to move into it.

Because the magician would not give up his 'relationship' with the toy, even though the being within had started to expand its reach, nothing could be done directly. You cannot force something in such a situation; you can only limit its expansion beyond the relationship between being and magician. The reach of the being started to badly affect another adept in the same community, so the adept took passive action.

He created a counterweight.

The adept stumbled across the same toy in a shop, but it was dressed as a consecrated bishop. He simply bought it and instructed the bishop toy to be the counterbalance to the feral toy. He sat it on a shelf in his home, and the problem slowly settled down.

It did not directly deal with the feral toy, as it was for its magical owner to do that in his own time. If you force such an issue, you end up with more mess than when you started. And you cannot solve all the problems triggered by thoughtless actions: the magician has to come to an understanding in their own time... or be slowly destroyed by their own stupidity. You simply stop the problem leaking to you, and then get on with your life.

You will find that the deeper you go in adept work, the more your focused magical ritual and visionary work is used for the big jobs.

Anything below this is dealt with by the power within you. Simple acts with intention—the right acts, relevant to the issue at hand—will deal with most minor and medium issues. The clue is knowing what acts are relevant and how to apply them. Always remember, little is better than lots, and poetic is better than full-on magical workings. Such poetic actions nudge a pattern into action that is already in place and waiting.

So, for example, back to the feral toy. As it grew as a vessel and a being moved in, that being became rooted, strong, and conscious. This triggered a shift in the patterns that began the formation of a threshold for a counterweight being to step in to keep things balanced. Because the toy was triggered by the magician's conversation and actions, the forming counterweight also needs the same trigger. When the adept got the bishop toy, he instructed it with intent and placed it in the magical household. This was a human trigger that invited the counterweight being to step over the threshold and into the waiting vessel.

Because the counterweight toy was a 'consecrated bishop,' the vessel had a certain function embedded within its shape and presentation. It could become what it looked like when uttered at. And remember that the counterweight being is the polar opposite of the parasitical being. It would not feed off people, it would not have sex—surprisingly, some bishops, even today, are celibate—and it has the religious connotations that work within the pattern of 'subduing demons.' It was the perfect choice. And it was amusing how the adept came across just such a toy when it was needed. Remember, things are put in your path to help you, and you will spot them if you pay attention. Or, I should say, you are nudged to visit places where the solution can be found.

A.5 Copper as deflection

Copper reroutes power and energy, not a decoy but a deflector and director. If a persistent flow of localized destructive energy, particularly if identified as coming in from a specific direction/source, using copper piping outside a property can deflect it and direct it down in the land.

A. Advanced Decoys

If the energetic disturbance runs on a defined path from A to B, usually spotted as a line of dying plants, you can put the pipes at both ends of the line. Simply knock the pipes in the ground so that they stand up, and they will channel the energy between them and in the ground.

Similarly if there are magical issues with the body on a particular side, wearing copper on that side can block it out. There are a lot of magical and medicinal uses for copper, usually for cleaning, containing or deflecting. Something kept within copper (like a pure copper box) will stay clean, and that has many different adept magical applications. But the strongest quality of copper from a magical perspective, is that it diverts and reroutes energy.

A lot of decoy work at an adept level is not flashy, but simple, effective and focused. However always remember that a good part of why it works is dependent upon the adept themselves and the magical patterns inherent within the adept. If you wish to deploy such methods for a none magical person or a student, ensure first that it will operate without you being present, or without it being reliant upon you to work. Otherwise you can end up being energetically drained as the decoy works for a student, or it just will not work which in turn puts the student at risk. Always use divination to check if you are not sure.

Appendix B

The prehistory of magical development: a series of unfortunate events

One of the important questions for an adept as they develop into their path as an adept magician, is why is magic here in the first place? How did it develop? Why did it develop? And what forms did it take? These questions and more are not really answerable in truth, as magic has existed probably for as long has humans have existed. However the process of asking those questions, and the process of research, thought and discovery leads us to a greater understanding of magic and of ourselves as magicians.

It is wise to be cautious when undertaking to find answers to such questions, as it can be tempting to try and fit history to our own narratives, which is an age-old problem where history is concerned. And again, it is unlikely we can totally avoid such overlays in our understanding, as we seek in relation to what we understand. But if we approach such exploration with as open a mind as possible, and also always look for the simplest and most reasonable explanations for what we find (as opposed to 'it's the aliens!') then it can lead us on a journey not only of historical learning, but of also self-discovery. Through looking at the struggles of our ancestors and what potentially drove them to magic, we can begin to understand our own limitations, fears and vulnerabilities.

The following essay is my own journey of discovery for the roots of magic in the northwest hemisphere, investigating what happened, how people reacted, how they organized themselves, and so forth. I also looked through the eyes of an adept magician, looking at magical responses to world events to see what I could recognize. The variations of magical responses are not endless, so we can as magicians sometimes see patterns of behaviour and magical action

B. The Prehistory of Magical Development: A Series of Unfortunate Events

that we recognize from today's magical actions and methods: humans really don't change that much over the millennia, and the same goes for the core elements of magic. I certainly found it a very interesting exercise, and it made me rethink a lot of assumptions I had made about our magical ancient ancestors.

★ ★ ★

And the light shineth in darkness: and the darkness comprehended it not

—*John* 1:5

To truly understand the emergence of the concepts that arise in today's Western magic, we have to cast our attention far back in time to the cradles that those concepts emerged out of. Those cradles emerged out of North Africa, Western Asia, the Near East/Caucasus, and Europe. To understand why those cradles emerged as they did, where they did, and what their focus was, we have to look at the conditions that those cradles emerged from. Religion and magic evolve from cause and effect, from our response as humans to the world around us.

If instead we only look back a thousand years for the roots of magic, we miss the point of the exercise. Finding such roots means looking far beyond the organized religions and magical practices of cultures that went before us. We need to look at what made our distance ancestors tick, at the cauldron of human thought and response to circumstance that birthed magic in the first place.

If we look at human nature in its barest form, we find two dynamics at play: find food, and store food. This is a base survival mechanism that, along with breeding and prey/predator behaviour, keeps our species alive. Those base mechanisms are still within us today as individuals and as societies: a lot of what we do has its roots in those basic survival instincts. Marketing in our modern consumer society taps into the 'find food/store food' mechanism that drives us: we buy, we consume, and we acquire more than we need (store/bank).

When it comes to the deeper spirit side of ourselves, we reach out to the unknown to try and make sense of the universe around us. We reach out for 'food' to eat for our souls and we try to store 'food' for our souls for the future (religion/beliefs). Magic is the active step that grew out of very early religious behaviour in its most primal form, where we move from passive acceptance of existence to a wish to actively engage with the universe around us and to have an element of control in how we navigate through life, not only in terms of survival, but in order to flourish.

B.1 Magic and its forms

Today, the same as a thousand years ago, magic falls into roughly two categorizes: secure resources, and clear the path ahead in our future (find food/store food). To secure resources (find food) magic developed into acts designed to attract, repel, bind and release: base actions to gain our needs and wants. Today we call this 'results magic' or 'low magic,' labels that are both confusing and not entirely correct.

These two labels are modern tags using modern language that both denigrate that type of magic and also limit the understanding of such magic. The term 'results magic' comes from a twentieth-century model of science, where experiments are designed and implemented not only to achieve results, but to make them repeatable in a stable manner. That is fine for science, but magic often does not work with such clearly defined parameters: it is as unpredictable as the weather. I strongly suspect that this term slid into use as an attempt to give magic modern credibility by using terminology more commonly used in science.

The same can be said of the term 'low magic': the term is loaded with snobbery and highhandedness. 'High magic' is a term used to describe magic that reaches into mystical exploration, whereas 'low magic' seeks to acquire something or stop something. I have tied myself in knots for years trying to explain my stance on this issue, and it is often assumed that I am hostile to 'results/low magic,' which is not the case. Rather, I see the gaping potholes and potential meltdowns that such magic can cause when it is paired with emotional immaturity, a modern consumer mentality, magical ignorance or incompetence, and a massive fragile ego. Magic is magic, and every type of magic has its place and function. The key is to understand what is appropriate and when. This type of magic

B. The Prehistory of Magical Development: a Series of Unfortunate Events

is about survival, about a person finding 'food' for their body and soul to keep them functioning, whatever they decide this 'food' is or represents.

'High' or mystical magic seeks the Divine in the universe: it moves beyond 'find food/store food' of 'low magic,' but in order to understand and work within that type of magic, 'low magic' must also be understood not only intellectually but practically: it is the weaving of inner power to manifest a controlled change in fate patterns. The magic itself (high or low) is no different be it mystical or functional: it is our approach and intention that creates a line of distinction.

This is a very important point to think about when looking into the ancient history of magic, as life in 7000 B.C. was very different to life today. The quest for mystical magic is a luxury in many ways: to embark upon such a journey of transformation and connection to the Divine, you need food in your stomach, a roof over your head and shoes on your feet. You need to be relatively safe and secure, and have time to ponder, think and act. It is those luxuries that mystical magic (and all mystical and philosophical thought) grew out of.

Functional (results) magic grew out of dire need, hence it is essentially folk magic: the magic of the ordinary person trying to get by in a way that they define for themselves. This is why it is more common in poor and rural communities both today and in the past. Simply understanding the dynamics of resources and human need can put a lot of magical history into perspective.

This is not to say that mystical magic did not exist in very ancient times. We have no books left to us from thousands of years ago, but what we do have is our magical knowledge of *today*. As a result, as practical working magicians, if we look deep into the ancient past then we will recognize certain acts that left archaeological findings for us to discover. We may not know the details, but the core magical mechanisms displayed in very ancient findings show both mystical and functional magical religious behaviour. It is through those behaviours that we can begin to understand ourselves as magicians today, and understand where our magic comes from.

When we look at ancient historical events that were happening at the same time as the emergence of magical behaviours, it can not only start to reveal to us the cause and effect of the development of magic, but it can also give us the foundational understanding of magical practice today: it becomes a whisper that travels down through time and reminds us of our magical roots.

In this essay, I wanted to dig back as far as possible to look for early magical behaviour. The timelines that I rummaged around in were far earlier than the written word, so I had to look at archaeological findings to see if I recognized anything. I also looked at the wider environment, at what we humans were doing and potentially why we were doing it.

This took me on a journey back to the period between 7000 B.C. and 5000 B.C. in human history, looking at what was happening with climatic events in the northern hemisphere from northern Europe to the Near East and north Africa. Bear in mind throughout this essay that I am not an archaeologist or trained historian, but I have done my best to check everything and ensure it is referenced.

B.2 The series of unfortunate events

The first thing that I tripped over was a rather startling bit of evidence from our genetic history. Sometime between the period of 7000 B.C. to 5000 B.C. modern humans experienced an abrupt genetic bottleneck specific to human males across the Old World.[1] Since the research paper was published in 2015, various other research bodies have tied themselves into knots trying to understand why this would have happened. Some theorized that it could be social (war, patrilineal dominance) and others suggested that it could be environmental (volcano). When there is a massive environmental disaster, often male fetuses abort[2], but the ratio of male to female in the bottleneck was 1:17, far greater than has been observed with spontaneous natural abortions during disasters.

But when scientists look at these startling anomalies, by nature of their focus, they tend to look for one specific potential cause, or a small orbit of potential cause and effect. However, when disasters

---

[1]Karmin, M. et al. A recent bottleneck of Y chromosome diversity coincides with a global change in culture. *Genome Res.* 25, 459–466 (2015).

[2]*Impact of earthquakes on sex ratio at birth*: Emek Doğer, Yiğit Çakıroğlu, Şule Yıldırım Köpük, Yasin Ceylan, Hayal Uzelli Şimşek, and Eray Çalışkan.

B. THE PREHISTORY OF MAGICAL DEVELOPMENT: A SERIES OF UNFORTUNATE EVENTS

strike, the ramifications can have wide and long-lasting effects in all aspects of society and health. So I spent some time looking closely at this time period to see what was going on, and I began to see the potential for complex cause and effect reactions in human populations across the Old World.

The period from around 6,500 B.C. to 5,000 B.C. reads a little like the title of a Lemony Snicket novel: *A Series of Unfortunate Events*. It was a rough time to be a human: for just over a thousand years, anything that could go wrong, did.

The picture that emerged was not one of a single massive disaster, but a series of them. It was a time of climate instability, and of massive land and environmental changes which would have likely affected various populations in a wide variety of ways. Let us look first at the natural events that occurred over that long period of time between 6,500 B.C. and 5,000 B.C., and then we will look at the fragments of evidence of the human responses to such upheavals, as they will give us a better picture of the cauldron within which what we know as magic today evolved, and why. Obviously magic existed in human cultures long before these events, but as we get further into this exploration of magical history, you will begin to see how pivotal this time was.

Leading up to the period we are looking up, we had the end of the last Glacial age around 10,000 B.C. and the beginning of the Holocene Thermal Maximum (9,000 to 5,000 B.C.).

Basically it went from cold to warm/hot, and such shifts cause all sorts of expansions and contractions in weather and the landscape. By the time we get to the era of the genetic bottleneck, things are really moving. Bear in mind that scientifically the following events can be dated only approximately, usually give or take a few hundred years.

The first event that caught my eye was the draining of Lake Agassiz: Ojibway, a vast glacial lake that at its peak potentially covered 440,000 square kilometres in the North American continent. Around 6,200 B.C. the vast fresh waters drained into the Atlantic, dumping a huge amount of fresh water down the Hudson Strait and into the Labrador sea west of Greenland. This is also thought to have caused or contributed to the collapse of the Laurentide Ice Sheet in

B.2. The series of unfortunate events

North America, which also dumped vast quantities of fresh water into the ocean. This is a crucial area for the global ocean circulation system, and such a massive influx of cold freshwater essentially stopped the Gulf Stream flowing.[1] It was rapid, and it was dramatic.

It caused absolute chaos around the world and is thought to have triggered what is known as the 8.2 kiloyear event, a period of intense rapid cooling that lasted anywhere from 200 to 400 years. It caused drier conditions in North Africa, and 300 years of aridification and cooling in the Near East/Mesopotamia/Western Asia. East Africa suffered 500 years of drought, and the effects/evidence of the rapid cooling have been found around the world.

Nature decided that this event was really just not dramatic enough, and decided to throw some spice into the mix, just to be sure. Around 6,225–6170 B.C. there was a massive landslip off the coast of Norway, known as the last Storegga slide, which dumped 3,500 cubic kilometres of debris into the north Atlantic, triggering a mega tsunami event. This event covered Doggerland, a land area that acted as a bridge between Britain, Denmark and the Netherlands. Doggerland was an area of expansive fertile hunting grounds for the region's Mesolithic cultures, and it vanished beneath the sea during this catastrophic event. It is likely that the area was already under extreme stress from rising seas from the 8.2 kiloyear event, and this massive tsunami had a huge impact on all the coastal communities of the North Sea. It has been approximated that the tsunami was thirteen feet high and went inland for fifty miles.

Around that time (6500–6200 B.C.) there was an apparent collapse of the eastern flank of Mount Etna that would have caused a potentially devastating tsunami that would have consumed Mediterranean coastal settlements. An Italian study led by Maria Pareschi of the Italian Institute of Geophysics and Volcanology in Pisa suggested the subsequent tsunami was possibly 130 feet high. If it was triggered by a massive volcanic explosion, it would have likely also caused a period of volcanic winter, as well as deep memories of a catastrophic event.

---

[1] *Reduced North Atlantic Deep Water Coeval with the Glacial Lake Agassiz Freshwater Outburst* Helga (Kikki) Flesche Kleiven, Catherine Kissel, Carlo Laj, S. Ninnemann, Thomas O. Richter, Elsa Cortijo. 2004 DOI: 10.1126/science.1148924

B. THE PREHISTORY OF MAGICAL DEVELOPMENT: A SERIES OF UNFORTUNATE EVENTS

The result of these different dramatic events would have had a massive impact on societies around the world as it suddenly got a lot colder—and in many places, dryer—with weather that was unpredictable, and massive floods in many areas. Thanks to archaeology, we know that there was a sudden interruption of the stability in society which is demonstrated in finds from Tell Sabi Abyad in Syria from this period of climate instability. Before the 8.2 kiloyear event, the pottery from Sabi Abyad was complex and highly decorative, and there was evidence of mass production and trading. Suddenly, around the 8.2 kiloyear event, the pottery ceased to be complex and decorative, and instead became rudimentary and simply functional. There was no evidence of decoration or trade: people were scrambling simply to survive and keep going.

The temperature began to rise steeply a few hundred years later with what is known as the Thermal Maximum, and with that came rising sea levels once again. Just as things were settling down, we have the Mount Mazuma eruption, a volcano in the Oregon segment of the Cascade Volcanic arc. Those eruptions sent a thirty mile high ash column into the stratosphere, with fallout over a three year period. The climatic eruption created Crater Lake, and it had a volcanic explosivity index of seven. It has been hypothesized that this mega explosion could have affected weather and temperature for three or four years in northern latitudes.

Two thousand years later we then have the 5.9 kiloyear climate event (Bond event 4, 3,900 B.C.) which triggered intense aridification to areas of North Africa and the Arab Peninsula, from which they never recovered. Incidentally, this is the most likely reason that people started to gravitate towards the Nile Valley from the nearby Sahara region.

It was also most likely the trigger for the North Atlantic cooling episode that brought about the decline and collapse of the European Neolithic culture in southeast Europe. The period from 4,200 B.C. to 3,900 B.C. saw intense climatic change with much colder winters in Northern Europe. The climate continued to deteriorate until approx. 2,800 B.C., and during this long span of time many settlements along the Danube were burned and abandoned, and overall the region saw an upsurge in settlement fortifications.

B.3 People and responses

When ancient cultures are subjected to repeated and prolonged extremes from natural disasters, and the stories of such disasters are handed down the generations in oral traditions, the response usually provokes two questions: 'what do we do?' (food, survival), and 'to whom or what do we pray for help?' The intense and sudden cooling of that period, with the accompanying weather extremes, will have put a lot of societies and communities under extreme stress. This was still a time where there was a mix of hunter gatherers, animal domestication, and early agricultural experiments.

Groups were already highly ritualized in their beliefs, and most religious finds we have from the archaeology of this period are continuations of 'Venus figures' (35,000—3,000 B.C.) and other anthropomorphic figures, along with other finds indicating the existence of bull cults. It is also pertinent to point out, at this stage of this essay, that highly ritualized behaviour was not, as has been previously presumed, the result of agriculture, but predates agriculture, or at least appears during the very early agricultural experiments before agriculture proper was established. It is likely that people's ritualized behaviour was focused on predator and prey: what threatened them, and what fed them.

The archaeological finds at Göbekli Tepe near Sanliurfa in southeast Anatolian Turkey of highly ritualized megalithic T-shaped decorated standing stones predate organized agriculture.[1] The deepest layers of the site show activity from the Epipalaeolithic period (18,000–8,000 B.C.) and the presence of megaliths from the Pre-Pottery Neolithic A period (PPNA). The samples used for dating were charcoal deposits and would have represented the endpoint of activity for that layer: the structures are older than the charcoal deposits. It is interesting to note that the images on the megaliths are predator and prey, with at least some of the megaliths attempting to portray humans: some of the T bars of the stones were fashioned as arms (but there are no heads).

This extensive ritual site, that was in use on and off for thousands of years, predated the first cultivation of the eight founder crops

---

[1]Schmidt, Klaus. (2000). *Göbekli Tepe, Southeastern Turkey. A Preliminary Report on the 1995-1999 Excavations.* Paléorient. 26. 10.3406/paleo.2000.4697.

B. THE PREHISTORY OF MAGICAL DEVELOPMENT: A SERIES OF UNFORTUNATE EVENTS

in the region. This is important to us as we dig around in the mists of pre-civilizations, as we are looking for cause and effect and ritualized behaviour that is the ancient forebear of magic. People didn't intentionally grow crops (agriculture) and then begin to civilize and ritualize: the ritualization came first.

The 'Venus' figures are very interesting in that they are depictions of females with exaggerated breasts and thighs, and sometimes vulvas. This depicts 'plenty' and 'breeding.' Remember that at the period we are looking at (between 7,000 and 5,000 B.C.) societies and populations in general were very small by today's standards. The focus would have been on three simple things: breed, find food, and store and protect excess food for winter. Everything would have focused around those three dynamics, and in a way, it still is today: we are driven to reproduce, to get what we need, and to obtain excess to store (bank accounts, etc.).

When there is a major disaster or a prolonged period of disasters like a climate collapse or shift, those three survival dynamics are put under extreme stress. Small populations are very vulnerable and can collapse easily. In such instances, the survival of females is far more important than the survival of males: if you have ten men and only one woman, only one child at a time can be born. If you have ten females and one male, ten babies can be born at one time: this ensures the continuation of the tribe into the future: it also causes a male DNA bottleneck. It is simple dynamics of nature, and one that we know was used in Neolithic societies.[1,2]

It is very likely that during this prolonged period of a few hundred years of rapid cooling (that then suddenly warmed back up a few hundred years later) that vulnerable communities began to collapse through cold, starvation, and lack of known resources. It is my theory that during this period not only were there natural spontaneous abortions, but also infanticide and male sacrifice. Culling/exposing the majority of male children would ensure that all meagre resources

---

[1] Birdsell, Joseph, B. (1986). "Some predictions for the Pleistocene based on equilibrium systems among recent hunter gatherers". In: Lee, Richard & Irven DeVore. *Man the Hunter*. Aldine Publishing Co. p. 239.

[2] Milner, Larry S. (2000). *Hardness of Heart / Hardness of Life: The Stain of Human Infanticide*. Lanham/New York/Oxford: University Press of America.

were protected and the small number of male children that made it to adulthood would then impregnate the females.

I was talking about this bottleneck and the culling hypothesis with a biologist who had specialized in genetics and epigenetics. She also suggested the possibility of castration as a survival mechanism. I was not aware of any evidence of eunuchs predating the first millennium B.C., where it was used in the courtly culture of the Neo-Hittite State of Carchemish[1]. I did some digging around and found evidence of knowledge of the link between testes and fertility in Neolithic animal husbandry (earliest findings approx. 5,600 B.C.): they castrated their surplus male animals to control breeding.[2] So that knowledge was kicking around the Old World and was very likely going on prior to the date of the archaeological finds. Castrating the majority of the living males while leaving fertile only the strongest and healthiest, though an extreme response, would make survival sense for the long-term population. But the castrated males would need to be fed in the short term, so I am not wholly convinced this could have been a solution, unless there was a need for working but infertile males.

It is very possible that the sudden bottleneck on the male DNA was a result of applying animal breeding knowledge to lower the male population, while also practising infanticide/exposure of male babies and the sacrifice of a percentage of the male adults. When you add to this the mix of disease, malnutrition (from extreme weather changes) and resulting resource wars, you get a picture of catastrophic change and extreme response from people in order for their tribe to survive.

Such events that spanned a few hundred years would have also stuck heavily in the ancestral memory, and stories of the events and how those events were dealt with would have gone down the generations in the forms of stories, oral history and ritual behaviour, something we know happened in Neolithic cultures.[3] I wonder if this

---

[1] Trevor Bryce: *The World of the Neo-Hittite Kingdoms: A Political and Military History.* Oxford, New York 2012

[2] *Size Reduction in Early European Domestic Cattle Relates to Intensification of Neolithic Herding Strategies.* Katie Manning, Adrian Timpson, Stephen Shennan, Enrico Crema University College Dublin Published: December 2, 2015 (Plos).

[3] *Oral Tradition and the Creation of Late Prehistory in Roviana Lagoon, Solomon Islands*: P. Sheppard, R Walter and S Aswani. Records of the Australian Museum, Supplement 29 (2004).

B. The prehistory of magical development: a series of unfortunate events

is the source of the stories that appear in various books of the Bible of killing first-born sons. There was certainly human sacrifice around at that time, and it carried on for another three thousand years.

One thing to note, as we look at this from the perspective of wanting to know how magical/ritual behaviour patterns formed and matured, is that human nature, mostly, doesn't change that much at its core.

The initial ritualized behaviour/actions are a direct response to a threat to survival. Once that threat has passed, the ritualized behaviour continues, not only because it gives people a sense that 'there is help out there if we get them on our side,' but also because it gives a sense of control. With that sense of control comes hierarchy, and with hierarchy comes more and more controlling actions in order to establish who should be where in the pecking order. Humans like to box and label things, to put their mark on things, and to be the 'one who knows' (hierarchy establishment).

Once you have a pattern of highly ritualized behaviour, you then have a situation where some will be better at it than others. Those with obsessive compulsive tendencies will seek to express them through their ritualized behaviour: that action needs me to do it with my left hand at this time and place, with my foot placed in a specific position, with a certain colour robe on, and I must bow three times before addressing the deity. This obsessive compulsive behaviour usually triggers first as a stress response before settling into a longer-term control response.

We see this sort of OC development in virtually every religion once it gets to a stable level of acceptance in a community: this is the early development of a priesthood and temple culture. Such development comes a long time after the initial catastrophe that triggered the actions in the first place, and often the true nature of the event loses its original identity as it morphs into mythology. The changing of a natural disaster into a mythic story can take many generations, but once established it can stay within a culture for thousands of years.

When we look at tribal societies today, often their mythology is clear enough that you can locate the original events that triggered the mythology. It becomes a story of remembrance, passed down

B.3. People and responses

orally from generation to generation, and the main reason for the continuance of the story is to learn its lessons: when there is a bad earthquake, head to the mountains because flooding is coming. This was very evident in the 2004 earthquake (9.3) and subsequent tsunami that struck on 26th December 2004.[1] I watched the TV with horror as the reporting unfolded over a series of days, and then with intense interest when a military head was being interviewed about the safety of the indigenous tribes that populate some of the Andaman Islands.

Through his connections with people in charge of protecting the tribes, many of which were isolated and not integrated with modern life, he managed to ascertain that the Shompens and Holschu tribes were totally unaffected by the event. The interpreter/warden for the tribes stated that 'the tribes fled to the hills before the tsunami struck': they knew it was coming. The knowledge that it was coming would have been linked to natural observations that are connected to their ancient stories. This was conveyed in a subsequent interview with one of the wardens: their mythology carried the information they needed to survive a disaster.

In societies that shift from hunter-gatherer to farmer, such a shift needs organization skills: someone has to measure the harvest, distribute, and also organize the workload. In the period of time that this essay is looking at, the communities we are looking at, i.e. the various cultures of the Old World, were mostly engaged in animal husbandry and early rudimentary agriculture with wild seeds. This societal structure facilitates organization, ritualized behaviour, and consequently a more sophisticated response to disaster and the subsequent development of mythology, ritual behaviour and so forth, as we have previously discussed.

The stories that come out of such organized ritual structure become increasingly steeped in mystique, as the communicator of that story in each generation needs to assert a sense of status and control over the people. Often the disaster stories become vehicles for asserting societal morality: if you are bad people, the mountain will blow, and only those special people who are priests can talk to

---

[1]The Hindu News December 31st 2004: *All Primitive Tribes Safe*. Article by Suresh Nambeth.

B. The prehistory of magical development: a series of unfortunate events

the mountain. And these are the ritual laws that you have to obey so that the mountain does not get angry.

This micro-controlling of actions, society rules, the organizing of ritual structures and behaviours, and the subsequent 'mystification' of the memory tales and mythology triggers the creation of behaviour that eventually develops into temple cultures.

At the timeframe that we are looking at, we see evidence of ' who do I ask for help' in the form of the anthropomorphic figures, the use of which spans thousands of years prior to the 8.2 kiloyear event and subsequent 5.9 kiloyear event. We also see the development of more sophisticated temple style behaviour with the creation and use of the megaliths at Göbekli Tepe: this appeared at the early phase of people trying to control their environment through animal husbandry and early agricultural experiments. The anthropomorphic figures found in Europe, for example the Löwenmensch (lion-human) figurine found in a German cave, which dates to around 35,000 B.C., and the animal images at Göbekli Tepe, tell us that the relationship between the animal and human kingdoms were of the utmost importance in terms of belief and ritualized behaviour, and had been for millennia.

After the series of unfortunate events in our timeframe of the 8.2 kiloyear event and subsequent fallout (the rapid climate changes, land instability, rising sea levels, and the male DNA bottleneck), we start to see a shift in ritualized behaviour. Remember that we can only draw conclusions from the archaeological evidence that we can access: the rest has to be hypotheses drawn from what we know of ritual behaviour, and what came later, as humanity in general is pretty predictable.

The shift in behaviour away from the animal/human relationship starts to emerge in the fifth millennium. This is when we start to see ritual enclosures that appear to have their focus upon the behaviour of the sun. This makes sense to us in that the sudden and intense drop in temperature of the 8.2 kiloyear event and the subsequent hundreds of years of climate instability and cold will have etched itself forever on the collective memory of the people. Just as that series of events faded deep into the recesses of ancestral memory, we then see the societies suffer once more with the resulting climate upheaval from the 5.9 kiloyear event and subsequent long-term cooling.

When the sun no longer does its job of always shining and always keeping us warm, when it has become unreliable, then you have to work to ensure that the anger of the sun does not return again. You want the sun to be as predictable as it used to be, to not get angry, and to bestow its favours upon you: crops, animals and human lives depend upon it.

This was also the time where people started to get rather serious about agriculture. The bounties of the land had become less dependable, the weather was constantly shifting and changing, and the resources were thinly spread. It made sense to have more control over your food supply by growing and storing it. In northern latitudes, with the shifting more towards agriculture, you would expect to see a shift in ritualized focus from predator/prey, to seasons, solar activity, and the appearance and vanishing of stars, as these tell you when to plant and when to harvest.

The rise in sites of solar observation and worship appears in the fifth millennium around the northern hemisphere. It is likely that such sites served multiple purposes: solar observation of the season through the alignment of the stones/solstices, a place for worship and sacrifice, and a place for tribal gatherings. This shift in focus from predator/prey/observation of the animal and plant kingdom, to a focus upon the sun and stars is a major turning point in humanity's magical thinking that would affect the development of magic for thousands of years. So it is worth a closer look: let us look at some of these early solar ritual centres, as a closer look at them raises difficult or at least interesting questions.

B.4 Early ritual solar circles

In the fifth millennium B.C., we start to see the appearance of enclosures and stone circles that are aligned to the movements of the sun. This is quite a radical change from 30,000+ years of animal/human centred ritual behaviour we have seen so far. Two of the earliest that have been found are Goseck Circle, Saxony-Anhalt,

B. The prehistory of magical development: a series of unfortunate events

Germany,[1] and Nabta Playa circle in Upper Egypt (in the desert 100 kilometres west of Abu Simbel).

The Goseck circle is thought to have been built around 4,900 B.C. and was in use for approximately two hundred years. It aligned with the winter solstice at sunrise and sunset, and the site has evidence of human sacrifice. The winter solstice is the lowest ebb of the sun in the Northern Hemisphere, and would have been a time when people feared the sun 'would not come back.' It makes sense that ritualized behaviour patterns emerged to time in with the winter solstice, and even today in some tribal societies, that behaviour continues.[2]

Later, stone circles aligned to the solar procession started springing up all over Europe and western Asia over a three-thousand-year period. The animals ceased to be the main focus, and the sun was the 'in thing' to watch and worship/ritually work with. A lot of these sites fell in and out of use over a long period of time, and quite a few of them have evidence of human sacrifice, or cattle sacrifice and of human burials (necropolis sites). The large quantity of cattle bones found at many of these sites is thought to indicate ritual sacrifice, but I would like to add something to that hypothesis that may throw a spanner into the works of those theories and also of mine.

When I lived for a while in a tribal society, when it got close to winter (October and November) the tribe would be very active with hunting, and extended families would gather together to collectively skin, and then dry the meat. The drying of the meat was often a family affair where everyone came together to butcher and dry the meat over huge hanging racks positioned over low ember fires.

This produced large quantities of dried meat that was then equally distributed between family members. It was a remembrance of survival mechanisms for a food supply that would last the harsh and bitter winters. No matter that there were supermarkets an hour away in a car, the drying of the meat was something still done as winter fast approached. It was also done, incidentally, upon the death

---

[1]François Bertemes, Peter F. Biehl, Andreas Northe, Olaf Schröder: Die neolithische Kreisgrabenanlage von Goseck, Ldkr. Weißenfels. In: *Archäologie in Sachsen-Anhalt*. NF Bd. 2, 2004

[2]Salizh/Pend d'oreille tribes on the Flathead reservation in Montana still practice 'Jump Dance,' a ritual nightlong stamping dance done around the time of the winter solstice to remind the sun to come back.

B.4. Early ritual solar circles

of a hunter. Meat would be dried and handed to the widow to ensure a food supply for the months ahead.

It is important to remember that as we look at these sites and their evidence, we do so from the comfort of a warm home that has a good food supply. We do not have the survival concerns that our ancestors did seven thousand years ago, so we tend to think only in terms of purely ritual behaviour, when often it was more likely that these behaviours served multiple purposes, including highly practical ones. And it is also pertinent to remember that these often highly practical acts worked well as survival and also bonding mechanisms, and they often persisted in closed and tribal societies right up to present day: if it works, why change it?

The second very early stone circle is a little more perplexing and is also far more relevant to us as magicians digging around in the underpants of history. Nabta Playa,[1] out in the Western Desert of Upper Egypt is an ancient centre of activity, with the first evidence of activity dating to around 10,000 B.C.. In the period between 6,500 and 5,000 B.C. we start to see a highly organized community with clear ritualized behaviour. The settlement had deep wells, organized 'streets,' and they appear to have been importing goats and sheep from western Asia. There is evidence of the ritual burial of cattle in stone roofed chambers lined with clay[2] (a very interesting parallel to the later burials of the Apis Bull in Egypt) and also of numerous large hearths (think about the drying of meat at collective slaughters).

The actual stone circle complex of Nabta Playa was thought to have been erected around 4,800 B.C., and there has been much debate about its meaning. It is clear that it aligns to the summer solstice, and is therefore a solar circle, but there have also been theories also about its alignment to various stars, namely the Orion constellation and Sirius. This theory was postulated by Wendorf, but later revised by University of Colorado (Boulder) astronomy professor J. McKim Malville. It is a complicated thing to work out what stars align to what stone circle, as there is the date consideration (the sky slowly

---

[1] Wendorf, Fred: Malville, J. McKim (2001) "The Megalith Alignments". In: *Wendorf, Fred: Schild, Romuald: Nelson, Kit, In Holocene Settlement of the Egyptian Sahara, vol. I, The archaeology of Nabta Playa.* New York: Kluwer Academic/Plenum.

[2] Wendorf, Fred: Schild, Romuald (November 26, 2000) *Late Neolithic megalithic structures at Nabta Playa (Sahara) southwestern Egypt.*

B. THE PREHISTORY OF MAGICAL DEVELOPMENT: A SERIES OF UNFORTUNATE EVENTS

processes) and also the fact that—and this is in the least scientific of terms—if you have a circle of stones, and a load of stars in the sky, then each stone or pair of stones will align to something. But it was and is very clear that the circle's layout of prominent stones aligned to the zenith of the sun at summer solstice.

I can understand a solar stone circle in northern Europe where the sun appears to be vanishing in the winter, but why were there solar stone circles in a land where the sun always shines? The authors of the archaeological study of Nabta Playa hypothesize that the site links to Sirius in connection with the rising of the Nile waters, and that the solar solstice is connected with the heavy rains that trigger the rising of the Nile. There are problems with that hypothesis.

The first problem is that the monsoon rains that feed the Nile inundation happen in Ethiopia and South Sudan, not Egypt, and those rains begin in late April/May, and appear in Aswan in July[1]. The other more obvious issue with the idea that this stone circle was a way of watching for the impending Nile inundation is its position and the terrain in which it was built. It was built at a time when that area was not desert: it was still lush and had a good water supply (and small lakes surrounding it). Its local inhabitants were pastoralists, and its position, most importantly of all, was 100 kilometres west of Abu Simbel: it was far away from the Nile, in an area that is now desert. What would be the reason for building a stone circle connected to the Nile so far away from it? And by pastoralists who did not rely on the Nile for their herds and rudimentary crops?

As an aside, the 'received wisdom' regarding the rise of Sirius, and the goddess Sopdet being connected to the impending inundation, now appears to be on shaky ground. The theory of connection between Sopdet (Sirius) and the Nile inundation was largely based upon an ivory tablet supposedly showing Sopdet and the Nile.[2] I looked at this tablet and struggled to see the connection, and upon further research I found this theory to have consequently been debunked by Egyptologists.

---

[1] https://www.britannica.com/place/Nile-River/Climate-and-hydrology

[2] Ivory tablet from the reign of Djer, First Dynasty.

B.4. Early ritual solar circles

I also came across a piece of research that closely looked at this supposed connection, and these researchers also tossed the theory out of the window based upon astronomical calculations across the time periods of Egyptian history: the inundation did not happen like clockwork and relied heavily upon the timing of the monsoon, which had variability. If the inundation was late, the Egyptians would add an extra month to their agricultural calendar. It is also pertinent to understand, if you look into this yourself and come across various popular sites, that the Egyptians had a solar *civil calendar* of 365 days, so their months processed around the seasons over time, as well as an *agricultural calendar* that started each year with the rising of the Nile. So in both calendars, the timing of the heliacal rising of Sirius slowly processed through the months over the millennia (today it rises in August). Often some of the websites confuse the Egyptian civil calendar with the agricultural one, so watch out for that mistake. Here is an excerpt of the research text that I found, that essentially debunks the theory.

Regarding the rise of Sirius and the Nile inundation:

> It is shown that the only text that describes this event is formulated very vaguely. It makes impossible to derive a reliable astronomical dating. Modern interpretations of this text are based on the free interpretation of the original source, and often do not match. According to historical evidence of Greek authors and later Egyptian texts, flooding of the Nile based on heliacal rising of Sirius could be predicted at the beginning of I millennium A.D.. This fact is confirmed by astronomical calculations.[1]

So we have a ritual centre inland from the Nile, that built up over thousands of years, and around 4,800 B.C. they built a stone circle that aligned with the summer solstice. Why? I find it fascinating that around the same time, in two very different locations (there could be more, we just don't know yet) people decided to build these ritual structures that focused upon the sun. They appeared (along with later subsequent ones scattered around the northern hemisphere) in the

---

[1] Heliacal rising of Sirius and flooding of the Nile: Nickiforov, M. G.: Petrova, A. A. *Bulgarian Astronomical Journal*, Vol. 18, No. 3.

B. The prehistory of magical development: a series of unfortunate events

very early days of agriculture, where animal husbandry was far more prominent.

The common theory about the rise of stone solar circles links to the seasonal cycles for agriculture, and yet, solar stone circles appear in such very different places with different seasonal structures: the summer solstice in the area that was to become Upper Egypt was very different in terms of agriculture and weather from the areas of northern Europe where other solar stone circles emerged at the same time. And keep in mind that we are talking about a time when the people who built these early structures were still, mostly, farming animals and harvesting wild seed.

We also must not forget that these early ancient peoples moved around a lot and travelled great distances: stories travel with people, ideas move around, and people copy what is different and cool, particularly if it appears to work. It is very likely that the huge and prolonged disturbances in climate, sea levels, and temperature affected those in more northerly climes far more severely than it did the people in the area that became Upper Egypt, but it would have affected them nonetheless. And if they encountered tales passed on along trading routes about the 'sun being angry,' those tales may have been scary enough, coupled with their own ancestral memory of a period of 'bad times,' and a renewal of those bad times, to prompt a shift to solar worship: there was also evidence at the Nabta Playa site of serious and prolonged drought (desertification from the 5.9 kiloyear event).

> Ra grew angry with mankind. He tore out one of his eyes, and threw it as Hathor down to earth, ordering her to destroy mankind. The goddess turned into the shape of a lioness, Sekhmet, and became the Lady of Pestilence and the Goddess of Vengeance. She was so successful at this, nearly wiping out the whole of humanity in her bloodthirsty killing spree, that Re grew alarmed and decided to put an end to the slaughter. He played a trick on Sekhmet: to quell her bloodlust he got her drunk on beer coloured like blood, and in her drunken stupor she forgot to continue killing, and transformed back into the gentle Hathor.

— The story of Sekhmet and the destruction of man, from the *Book of the Holy Cow*.

B.5 Chambered tombs in Northern Europe

In the colder, more seasonal north we see a continuation and development of the ditch/enclosure circles that developed into large and complex stone alignments. In both cooler and also warmer climes, we have evidence of human sacrifice, usually at high status burials in the warmer climes, and at the solar circles in colder climes.

From 4,200–3,900 B.C. in Europe we see continued climate instability, with the 5.9 kiloyear event (3,900 B.C.) with once again rapid cooling and intense cold winters.[1,2] Once again we see a ritualized response to this dramatic change and harsher living conditions.

Britain around the time period of 4,000 B.C. to 3,500 B.C., from a ritual cultural perspective, appeared to have focused upon two things: solar precession and death (sounds very Egyptian!). It is during this period that we find the chambered tombs:[3] complex stone constructions that housed one or more bodies. By approximately 3,000 B.C., stone circles and alignments were cropping up in various places in northwestern Europe and the tradition continued for another two thousand years.[4]

One of the major themes in magical history can be found in the ancient Dynastic Egyptian culture, and that is the theme of death and the afterlife. The sun and the progression of the soul through death and the Underworld are major themes in ancient Egyptian theology: the souls of the dead undertake a series of 'tests' as they travel through the Underworld, and at times they rest in caverns of

---

[1]Bond, G.: et al. (1997). "A Pervasive Millennial-Scale Cycle in North Atlantic Holocene and Glacial Climates." *Science* 278 (5341): 1257–1266. doi:10.1126/science.278.5341.1257.

[2]Bond, G.: et al. (2001). "Persistent Solar Influence on North Atlantic Climate During the Holocene." *Science* 294 (5549): 2130–2136. doi:10.1126/science.1065680.

[3]Pearson, Mike Parker (2005). *Bronze Age Britain (Revised Edition)*. London: B.T. Batsford and English Heritage.

[4]Burl, Aubrey (2000). *The Stone Circles of Britain, Ireland and Brittany*. New Haven and London: Yale University Press.

B. The Prehistory of Magical Development: A Series of Unfortunate Events

the Underworld until it is time for them to release and rejoin their journey of development through the Gates of the Duat.[1] The light that guides the souls on their path of development and awakening is the light of Re, the sun as it travels in the Underworld.

With that in mind, the chambered tombs in the British Isles are worthy of a look. Of the many chambered tombs that litter the British Isles, there are three that are worthy of inspection as good examples.

The first is Newgrange (Brú na Bóinne) in the Boyne Valley, Country Meath, Ireland.[2] It is a large, impressive passage-chambered tomb from the Neolithic era (3,200 B.C.). It is aligned with the winter solstice, so that sunlight at that time flows through a 'roof box,' an opening that allows sunlight to flood the inner chamber at the winter solstice. When it was opened, human remains and grave goods were found, so it was definitely used as a tomb. There are quite a few chambered tombs in Ireland that align with the winter solstice. So here we have burials, placed in 'caves' (Underworld) where the sun at its lowest in the year falls into the cave and lights it up.

The second of interest is Bryn Celli Ddu in Anglesey, Wales.[3] It also dates to the Neolithic period and post hole remains that have been carbon-dated show activity from around 4,000 B.C.. It started out as a henge within a stone circle and later was developed as a chambered tomb mound. It is aligned to the summer solstice, unlike many others that align to the winter solstice, and it makes me wonder if the different alignment is a throwback to its earlier days as a stone circle/ditch. This would make sense with the much earlier circles we looked at earlier.

What caught my eye in particular was a serpent stone that is in the mound. When the mound was opened up, a 'patterned stone' six and a half feet high was found buried under the mound: the shape of the carving was very reminiscent of the later depictions in ancient Egypt of the 'Mehen' serpent that protects the solar god Re as he traverses the Underworld.

---

[1]Sheppard, McCarthy, Littlejohn (2017) *The Book of Gates*. Quareia Publishing UK ISBN 978-1911134220.

[2]O'Kelly, Michael J. 1982. *Newgrange: Archaeology, Art and Legend*. London: Thames and Hudson.

[3]Yates, M.J.: Longley, David (2001). *Anglesey: A Guide to Ancient Monuments on the Isle of Anglesey*. Third edition. Cardiff: Cadw.

B.5. Chambered tombs in Northern Europe

The Bryn Celli Ddu serpent stone was dug out and stood back up where the excavator thought it would have stood when the henge was active, so its original placing within the chamber is unknown. The theme of Underworld spaces, serpents, and the sun in the Underworld is an ancient and persistent motif in various places in the North hemisphere. It was also a strong theme in ancient Egyptian theology, with the Underworld populated by many serpents (e.g. Apep, Mehen, uraei, etc.) some of whom were helpers to the human souls, and some who were archenemies.

The third chambered tomb, Maes Howe,[1] on Mainland Orkney, Scotland, is truly astonishing and was very likely not a tomb at all. It is a vast chambered 'tomb' where the rear wall illuminates at the winter solstice. When it was opened, there were no grave goods and no human remains: it was never used for burial and was likely a ritual chamber. Once again, we have the 'cave' where the winter sun at its lowest shines into the 'cave' casting its light into the darkness.

This pattern of the light of the sun shining into the darkness at the darkest part of the year has magical parallels to one of the deep mysteries in magic: the light of the sun falling upon the seeker in the darkness of the Underworld, as they start the long journey up out of the darkness and up to the stars: the path of mystical ascent. It is one of the most prominent themes today in mystical magic: could this early ritualized behaviour be the far distant ancestor of today's magical mystical theme of ascent/rebirth from the darkness?

We have no way of knowing if this deep and ancient part of the Magical Mysteries was indeed what these ancient people were working with, or whether it is a total coincidence: were they simply copying the ebb and flow of the sun through the seasons, particularly in light of the harsher winters they were suffering? That is the usual hypothesis that is put forward, and yet we see the same pattern emerge in countries that do not, and did not, have such distinctive winters.

As a magician, I can say that these powerful dynamics and patterns are inherent within the magical human consciousness, not because magicians have been told it is, but because that is what

---

[1]Renfrew, Colin (editor) (1985). *The Prehistory of Orkney B.C. 4000–1000 A.D.*. Edinburgh: Edinburgh University Press.

B. The Prehistory of Magical Development: a Series of Unfortunate Events

you experience in vision when you tread the magical mystical path, regardless of what you 'know' or don't know of historical patterns. A person going through deep magical development will experience these patterns in some form whether or not they have been exposed to the concepts.

But that then also poses a very interesting magical question: did these inner presentations that magicians stumble across in vision arise naturally, as organically forming structures of consciousness, or are they imprinted upon the collective inner consciousness of humanity because they have been purposefully worked with, in a visionary and ritual sense, for millennia, and have thus formed as a created inner structure? Did the various dramatic climate events first cause an outer social and ritual response, and then a deeper inner magical response, which in turn created inner visionary experiences that persist in human consciousness to this day?

The swimmer in the Nu is one with the darkness and silence. The swimmer does not know he is a swimmer: he is, and is within, the Nu. The golden rays of Re fall upon the swimmer, lighting up what was within the darkness. The swimmer reflects the light of Re, and thus is no longer one with the Nu.[1]

Excerpt from the Egyptian *Book of Gates*, Ninth Gate, Scene 58:

> O those being filled, who are in the water, The swimming/golden/molten, who are in the Nu, Look upon Re who is passing through, In his barque which is great of Mysteries. Now he ordains the design of the Gods: Now he formulates the business of the Radiant. Oho! Stand up, ones who are in the Nu: Behold Re as he ordains your designs.
>
> Says to them, Re:
>
> A coming forth for your heads/best, those who are diving, Plying for your arms, those who are slack, Swiftness for your hurrying, those who are swimming/golden/molten, Breath for your noses, those who are expanded. A coming into power for you through your water, Be you at peace in your cold refreshment. Your setting out is in the Nu,

---

[1] J McCarthy. (2018). *The Quareia Apprentice Study Guide* ISBN 9781911134329.

B.5. Chambered tombs in Northern Europe

Your strides are of a stream. Your Presences, which are on earth, they are at peace, Meaning they breathe, and there is no destruction for them.

Their extension is the peace of the Earth.

Now, putting forth what is theirs on Earth Means coming into the power of one's peace on Earth.[1]

The above quote is taken from the *Book of Gates*, a ritual funerary text from New Kingdom Egypt. The *Book of Gates* first appears (so far as we know today) in fragments during the end of the eighteenth dynasty (approx. 1323 B.C.) and is the ritualized passage of Re (Solar deity) through the twelve hours and gates of the Underworld. It appeared on royal tomb walls, and also in fragments upon the golden sanctuary of King Tutankhamun.

Copyright © Josephine McCarthy 2018: all rights reserved.

---

[1] Sheppard, McCarthy, Littlejohn (2017) *The Book of Gates.* Quareia Publishing UK ISBN 978-1911134220.

Quareia
a New, Free School of Magic
for the 21st Century

*Advancing education in Mystical Magic
and the Western Esoteric Mysteries.*

www.quareia.com
schooldirector@quareia.com

Quareia is a practical magical training course founded by Josephine McCarthy and Frater Acher. It is a complete and freely available course designed to develop a student from a complete beginner into an adept. There are no barriers to entry: the course is accessible regardless of income, race, gender, religion, or spiritual beliefs.

Quareia is aligned to no particular school or specific religious, mystical, or magical system; rather it looks at and works with various magical, religious, and mystical practices that have influenced magical thinking in the Near Eastern and Western world from the early Bronze Age to the present day.

The entire course is free and openly available on the Quareia website.

www.ingramcontent.com/pod-product-compliance
Lightning Source LLC
Chambersburg PA
CBHW071731080526
44588CB00013B/1987